RECLAIMING YOUR BEST SELF

CHASITY K. ADAMS, PSY.D.

RECLAIMING YOUR BEST SELF

The Four Disciplines of Mindful Acceptance

CHASITY K. ADAMS, PSY.D.

RECLAIMING YOUR BEST SELF: THE FOUR DIS-
CIPLINES OF MINDFUL ACCEPTANCE
Copyright © 2017, Chasity K. Adams, Psy.D.

The names, details, and circumstances described in this
book are based on real experiences but might have been
changed to protect privacy. This publication is not a sub-
stitute for the advice of health care professionals.

Unless otherwise indicated, all quotations from the Christian Bible are paraphrased, not following a published edition.

www.shaperquill.com

Acknowledgements

I would like to thank my parents for being my biggest fans, confidants, and friends. I especially want to thank my mother for instilling in me a strong work ethic and her unrelenting faith in my will to succeed.

I would like to thank my daughters, Jade and Amber, for teaching me patience, selflessness, and unconditional love.

I would like to thank my husband, Anthony, for his confidence in my skills and support. Thanks for believing in me.

I would like to thank everyone who read my manuscript in the early, unpolished stages, and all my beta readers, particularly those who read my manuscript over and over while it was in the beginning stages: Dr. Tiffanie Robinson, Jennifer Jones, Charu Khamuria, Cortney O'Neal, and Marlene Gibbs.

I would like to thank my editor, Dr. Nathan Barnes, for believing in my project, mentoring me during my writing journey, and providing me with author insights.

I would like to thank everyone who has ever encouraged or prayed for me.

Contents

PREFACE

T HE PRACTICE OF SELF-CARE is important to our overall well-being. Most people associate self-care with grooming and physical care. Emotional self-care focuses more on the mind and emotions rather than our physical bodies. Simply put, it is care for the inner Self that spills over to our physical self. It would be impossible to practice emotional self-care behaviors while ignoring the importance of our physical shell.

Emotional self-care is intentional work that invites us to prioritize our emotional wellness and happiness as a way to live as our Best Self. As a form of emotional self-care, I encourage you to consider the four disciplines of Mindful Acceptance. It is an active approach that I developed from *acceptance and commitment therapy* (ACT), an evidence-based, values-driven, behavior change therapy.

Mindful Acceptance is a psychological form of emotional self-care that begins in the mind, allowing every situation *to be what it is* (especially when we cannot change or control it), and its result is value-driven action. This approach to life is useful to us because we can't change or control most internal and external situations. Regarding our internal landscape, we can be intentional about choosing and focusing on thoughts that are motivating, positive, and realistic. We can have some agency in our external world by engaging in behaviors that are appropriate and productive, such as leaving toxic relationships or changing jobs. Mindful Acceptance encourages us to surrender to the present moment, allows us to clearly see a given situation for what it is, and empowers us to choose the best possible response.

These four disciplines encourage us to take action on behalf of what we want out of life. While creating a mental environment of positive and realistic thoughts, Mindful Acceptance encourages us to practice habits of happiness. The more we practice and engage in specific behaviors, the greater chance that we can create healthy habits that are conducive to happiness. Positive habits can be formed as long as we are intentional about practicing daily habits of happiness.

I encourage you to learn how to get in touch with your Best Self by engaging in Mindful Acceptance, which is a flexible approach to relating to one's Self, others, and the world. The practice of Mindful Acceptance will help you engage in emotional self-care, which is care for your total Self: mind, body, and spirit.

If we focus on reclaiming our Best Self by practicing emotional self-care and embracing Mindful Acceptance, we can experience the freedom of self-sufficiency, psychological flexibility, and interpersonal effectiveness. Our relationships with ourselves and other people will be more fulfilling, constructive, and mutually beneficial when we live everyday as our Best Self.

Part 1

BEGINNING WITH THE SELF

FLYING WAS FUN AND STRESS-FREE before my children came along. All I had to do to have a good flight was avoid the dreaded middle seat. I must admit that over time, I began to tune out the flight attendants' words as they repeated the same instructions that I heard every time I flew. Find your exit doors; only sit by those doors if you're physically able to open them. The seat becomes a flotation device. Put on your oxygen mask before helping your neighbor. *Blah, blah, blah.*

After having children, flying would never be the same. A particular section of the safety instructions that I had once ignored had new meaning for me the first time that I flew with my young children next to me. My ears perked when the flight attendant said, 'Put on your oxygen mask before trying to help others around you.' My immediate response was *absolutely not*! My mind began to race. I must take care of my children! How could I refuse help to someone whom I love, selfishly focusing on saving myself when a loved one is in need?

Fortunately, the instructions for airline passengers aren't designed to keep us from helping our children. In fact, what we are doing is taking care of ourselves so that we can better help them. We need to put on our own oxygen mask before we are able to help loved ones. A mother who refuses to put her oxygen mask on first will pass out before she can help her children. Our life and the lives of our loved ones depend on us taking care of our Self first.

EMOTIONAL SELF-CARE

WHEN I ASK MY CLIENTS, workshop participants, and social media audiences about different types of self-care, they mention exercise, nutrition, taking prescription medications, and getting enough sleep. Physical aspects of self-care are absolutely critical for physical and emotional health, but most people ignore their emotional needs.

Exercise, as a form of self-care, is as an elixir for many physical ailments. I won't delineate the many benefits of exercise. I underscore the importance of exercise as a form of emotional self-care because of its impact on our mood. Exercise can have a similar benefit as antidepressants, such as reducing anxiety and depression, but without the nasty side effects. Exercise releases endorphins that give us a natural high, and for most of us, it feels good. Don't you want to feel good? Well, exercise is a quick and dirty method of feeling good. It is a good emotional self-care practice because it has a positive effect on our emotions.

Emotional self-care focuses more on the mind, emotions, and soul. Simply put, it is care for the inner Self. Unfortunately, most of us do not make emotional self-care a priority. Some people think that emotional self-care is selfish, preferring to give priority to the emotional needs of others. We are so often caring and doing for others that we forget about caring and doing for ourselves. We care for our children, parents, spouses, clients, patients, co-workers, and friends. When do we care for ourselves? 'Not often enough' is the response that I hear from friends, family, workshop participants, social media followers, and clients. That response prompted me to begin research for this book. It is our responsibility to value our own emotional wellness. We need to increase awareness and take ownership for our needs and not expect others to prioritize them for us.

When we expect others to prioritize our emotional self-care, we set ourselves up to blame the other person for our unhappiness. Blame is a distraction from the real issue at hand, which is within ourselves. Blame gives people, places, and things the power to control our inner peace and happiness. At the same time, we need to allow other able-bodied adults to handle, manage, and take ownership for their own well-being. Let's not attempt to take away other people's power over their own lives. The wonderful news is that when we are able to take care of ourselves and our own needs, we are better able to take care of others in an appropriate and healthy manner.

Making time for your Self

WE TEND TO GET SO SUBMERGED in doing, managing, and dealing with other people and their problems that we neglect our Self. Stephen R. Covey, in *The 7 Habits of Highly Effective People*, reminds us that we need to 'put first things first.' Prioritizing what you need is different from prioritizing your wants and desires. We need a healthy amount of selfishness that demonstrates that we love ourselves enough to 'put first things first,' by letting go of the people, places, and things that are not working for us.

How can you share your Self if there isn't enough of you to share?

HEALTHY SELFISHNESS LOOKS NOTHING like the narcissistic person who has an inflated and grandiose personality that masks internal deficiencies. I suggest that you challenge the belief that you *should* be selfless at all costs and explore what it feels like to prioritize your own emotional self-care, which is healthy and rewarding to you and those around you. How can you share your Self if there isn't enough of you to share?

The practice of emotional *self*-care is *selfless*. Wayne W. Dyer, in *Your Erroneous Zones*, suggests that people who prioritize their self-care are less selfish than people who do not. When we are taking care of our own emotional needs, we are reframing situations in order to reduce negativity, asking for what we need from others, soothing our own wounds, and seeking support when needed. Specifically, we are not burdening others with our own sensitivities and emotional issues that we are responsible for handling. People who do not have an effective practice of emotional self-care behave insecurely, engage in negative self-talk, practice the habit of worry, and bombard others with needy behaviors.

Taking care of your Self

EMOTIONAL SELF-CARE BY NO MEANS IMPLIES that we do not care for the welfare of others. I am not suggesting in any way that we neglect or harm others. The take-home message is to accept responsibility for our own emotional wellness and do what we need for ourselves in order to rejuvenate and revitalize. We are able to give more to others, and the world when we operate as our Best Self.

Some people drain their emotional energy by taking care of the needs of others before taking care of themselves. Low emotional energy will leave these folks at risk for resentment.

KAREN'S BEHAVIOR underscored the negative effects of self-neglect in relationships. She was very nice and just wanted someone to love her. Karen fell hard for Dave. She deeply wanted to be in a meaningful relationship and did whatever it took to get Dave to commit to her.

Karen invested a lot of time, energy, and resources into Dave. She justified her behavior to her friends by saying that she loved him. She was always available when he needed her to take care of something for him, which was often. She helped him rent cars when his car would break down. She loaned him money when he was short on bills. Karen even provided him with luxurious meals and outings.

Over time, Karen found herself feeling bitter and sullen. She was broke, overweight, and miserable. Karen battled within herself about why she put up with Dave, which only made her feel worse. Eventually, Karen arrived at the point where she resented how Dave was treating her, and she lost the energy to continue to give to him. Dave responded by breaking off all communication. Karen was devastated. After the break-up, she took Dave to small claims court in an attempt to recover some of her finances. This relationship lasted far too long because emotional self-care wasn't a priority.

The practice of emotional self-care enables us to care for ourselves so that we can better help others. We must put on our oxygen mask before we are able to help loved ones. If you don't put on your oxygen mask, you will be unconscious and useless to anyone around you, including the people whom you love deeply. Our lives and the lives of our loved ones depend on us taking care of ourselves first, which begs a question.

Discovering the Self

WHO AM I? Am I what I do? Am I what I like? Am I the sum of my behaviors? Am I the thoughts that consume me? Who am I?

The answer can only be found in a state of pure awareness, which lies dormant and observing under the identities that we have created for ourselves in order to survive in a world that does not tolerate differences. If you are confused about your deepest Self, ask yourself what you would be doing today if you were truly free. This question will help you get in touch with what you really want for your life. Personal freedom implies liberty from the approval of others, guilt, worry, fear, self-doubt, and insecurity.

Who are you? You are love. You are life, sentient, and connected to all living forms. You have thoughts that you can choose to embrace if they work for you. You have different *selves* or personalities that you can flexibly select based upon a situation and your values. Your different selves and personalities are not truly discrete selves, but culminations of learned and automatic behaviors.

Your 'mind' includes all the intentional, positive, and workable thoughts that you have created. You have automatic thoughts that are outside your awareness and often contrary to your character. You are much greater than the sum of your thoughts. The thoughts in your head are composed of your temperament, prior learning, cultural influences, and mental representatives. All humans experience unwanted thoughts and emotions that do not define who they are. You are not your thoughts! You are the *noticer* and observer of your thoughts.

Your Best Self

A SURE WAY TO GET WHAT YOU WANT out of life is to focus energy, attention, and actions on embracing your Best Self. Your Best Self will emerge when you experience freedom from past hurts, self-defeating beliefs, and automatic behaviors. Your Best Self can flexibly choose thoughts and behaviors that are aligned with your values without undue influence from your past or others. Your Best Self is true to your values by being courageous and doing what matters in the face of discomfort and ambiguity. You are living as your Best Self when your happiness, peace, and serenity are under your control.

Every day, strive to behave as the Best version of your Self. Put mental and physical energy into engaging in behaviors that make a difference in your life and the lives of others. Be mindful of the games that the mind likes to play. You may experience a day in which your mind wants you to believe that you did not behave as your Best Self. Your mind may want you to believe that you were your Worst Self. The mind likes to play the all-or-nothing game: you were either your Best Self or your Worst Self. Don't buy into it.

Commit to doing your best every day. If you have done your best, at the end of the day, be intentional about reminding yourself that you did your best and it was good enough. Your Best Self cannot be judged when you are operating within your value system. Don't get caught up in the games your mind likes to play. Recognize the game and choose not to play it.

Many people get stuck in trying to figure out their authentic selves. People spend too much time searching in their minds for their true Self and not enough time doing things that will lead them towards being their Best Self. Your authentic Self may change periodically, which could cause confusion and stagnation. One situation may call for you to behave authentically in one way, and another situation may call for you to behave authentically in an opposite manner.

The hallmark of our Best Self is that it is flexible and adaptable to the situation. Our Best Self is resilient and persistent. Successful people know how to embrace their Best Self and get the job done. Start practicing and cultivating Best Self behaviors today!

Crying for help

A 2-YEAR-OLD GIRL HAS A TANTRUM on the floor at the grocery store. Innocent shoppers can almost hear the mother's inner Self cry for help as they maneuver their carts around the screaming toddler. Some people offer words of sympathy, but everyone sees that a mother cannot control her child. Is she a bad parent? Doesn't she know that the child may need food, a nap, or some discipline? Why doesn't the mother care for her child? Children don't just throw fits for nothing. *Is the child being abused?*

The mother can panic, wondering what people think of her as a parent. Frustrated, she quickly evaluates her choices. Does she wait patiently for her child's tantrum to pass? Does she snatch up her child and leave the grocery store, abandoning her groceries?

What if she could choose how to experience this normal part of life without being debilitated by negative thinking? Her thoughts are not the problem. Her thoughts are just doing what thoughts do as a problem-solving mode of mind: they attempt to solve the apparent problem. As an alternative to being hijacked by her thoughts, this mother has a power within that can increase her ability to make the best decisions in this moment. This mother could benefit from observing her thoughts as a way to turn off autopilot and turn on intentional thoughts and behaviors. Intentional thoughts include:

- I'm doing the best that I can do in this moment.
- This too shall pass.
- I can do this!
- It's perfectly natural for babies to have tantrums!

MINDFUL ACCEPTANCE OFFERS FOUR DISCIPLINES that can liberate people from irrational and unhealthy thoughts. These disciplines are ways of being—mindful, intentional, creative, and self-compassionate. As ways of being, these disciplines often overlap and can be applied situationally and contextually according to whatever challenges we face.

Mindful Acceptance is an approach to life that begins with an awareness of things the way they are, which is the principle at the heart of *mindfulness.* Many thoughts and situations are simply beyond our control. People will think what they will think about a parent with a screaming child. If you are the parent of the screaming child, practice creative self-talk by saying to yourself, 'So what? Who cares?' While a toddler is crying about the end of the world, adults can be mindful of the thoughts racing through their minds. You can allow your automatic thoughts to come and go like people walking by in New York's Central Park.

We may involuntarily think that our crying child is a sign that we are an incompetent parent, but we can simply be *mindful* and allow that thought to be what it is rather than taking any sort of automatic action based on it. We can then apply the other three disciplines of Mindful Acceptance. By being *self-compassionate*, we are affirming that we are doing the best that we can do, despite our initial thoughts. We can be *intentional* about increasing thoughts that can help us reassess and regroup in the moment rather than overreact. Finally, we can be *creative* about handling situations in constructive ways.

If we choose to adopt Mindful Acceptance as an approach to dealing with life, we will be empowered to experience a meaningful and purposeful life, engage in healthy relationships, love and accept all aspects of ourselves, and spend more time in the present moments of life. When we are practicing Mindful Acceptance, we are preparing ourselves for all the many opportunities, successes, and rewards that the Universe will make available to us.

Mindful Acceptance is an intentional acknowledgement of what is not within our power to change or control, such as a past event, our natural temperament, or another person's behavior. There are many aspects of a two-year-old's tantrum that are beyond anyone's control. Two-year-olds are wild and many of our internal responses are involuntary. The mother may be embarrassed, but she doesn't need to beat herself up for her less than perfect parenting moments. Shoppers may want to silence the little girl by any means necessary, but they can happily continue with their day.

Most of us have seen a toddler throw a fit in front of strangers in a grocery store; we are intimately familiar with the tiny cry for help when we need to be patient with screaming children. It happens, and everyone will have an emotional response to it. Fortunately, we aren't our emotions, and we can choose to be mindful of our inner life and be self-compassionate, intentional, and creative in every life situation. The practice of Mindful Acceptance as a form of emotional self-care will help you stop running from unpleasant emotional responses and start taking care of your Self.

Reclaiming your Best Self

THE FIRST PART OF THIS BOOK examines the Self, focusing on our Best Self, and the second part addresses our relationships with other people. Focusing on the Self, I first highlight that our emotions, perspectives, thoughts, and successes begin in our minds. True happiness depends on what we can control—our responses to our inner and outer life—and not on what we cannot control (such as the opinions of other people). Then, I break down the concept and benefits of Mindful Acceptance. From there, I move on to presenting six gifts of emotional self-care, highlighting the benefits of adopting healthy self-care habits, which are habits of happiness. Part 1, which focuses on the Self ends with an emphasis on living fully in the present.

The second part of the book focuses on interpersonal relationships. This section begins with how we can use Mindful Acceptance to enhance our interactions on social media, help other people effectively, and practice forgiveness. Many relationships can be dramatically improved or ended at the right time when we know our roles, stop expecting our significant other to read our minds, and when we are mindful that almost all situations are transitory. Finally, I address how Mindful Acceptance can free folks from fear-based parenting and serve as a model for healthy parent-child relationships.

Reclaiming Your Best Self is designed to help you practice Mindful Acceptance as an approach to living a full, healthy, happy, and meaningful life. This book will encourage you to practice unconditional self-love and acceptance so you can finally be comfortable in your own skin.

There is a Best Self in Action exercise at the end of the chapters designed to help increase mindfulness, self-compassion, intentional behavior, and creativity. The practice of Mindful Acceptance is intensely practical; it isn't just a lofty idea. It will increase your awareness and encourage you to reevaluate your current relationships and make decisions that are in your best interest and consistent with your values.

WHEN I FLY WITH MY KIDS, I am fully prepared to put my oxygen mask on before I try to take care of them. I know that like everyone else, I must take care of my basic needs before I can take care of others, even my kids. The same thing is true for my emotional well-being: I must love and accept myself before I can be the best wife, mother, and psychologist.

People who engage in emotional self-care are happier, healthier, and kinder to others. When we have worked on our Self and we are full of self-acceptance and self-love, we have the emotional freedom and capacity to genuinely love and care for others. Emotional self-care helps us to better care for others. The four disciplines of Mindful Acceptance will enable you to take care of others without losing emotional consciousness.

2

IT BEGINS IN THE MIND

WHY CAN'T I STOP THINKING ABOUT my recent break-up? What's wrong with me? How could I have done things differently? Why do I keep picking the same kind of guy? I must not really want a healthy relationship. Why can't I just stop thinking about her? Why is this coming to my mind? I just want to stop thinking about it!

In *The Happiness Trap*, Russ Harris suggests that our minds have two metaphorical parts: the observing self and the thinking self. The *observing self* is the silent, nonjudgmental watcher of our thoughts and emotions that is unaffected and untouched by external factors. Our observing self has been with us since birth and will continue to be with us until we die. This sense of Self is the *noticer* of our thoughts and sensations. It does not judge, evaluate, compare, or analyze. The simple act of observation creates a distance between our Self and our thoughts, which allows us to be intentional about thinking, 'It is what it is.'

The observing self allows us to notice our thoughts without being our thoughts.

OUR OBSERVING SELF is our most consistent, courageous, and deepest Self. The observing self provides us with the subtle strength to sit with ambiguity, anxiety, and fear without being overwhelmed and moved to impulsive or avoidant behaviors. Being in close contact with our observing self allows us to embody and embrace our Best Self.

The *thinking self* is responsible for the excess judgments, comparisons, labeling, criticizing, and analyzing that occur in our minds. The thinking self is the background music in our minds that never turns off. It is always present, and it becomes louder when we are addicted to giving it attention and energy. The best way to deal with the thinking self is to acknowledge our stream of consciousness and become intentional about not engaging with unwanted thoughts. When you wonder why your mind keeps bringing up a situation, consider this: because it wants to.

Sometimes, the thoughts that go through our minds are irrational, illogical, and random. However, there often is some logical content that triggered the illogical cascade. Don't allow the logical content of your thoughts trick you into becoming one with your flow of thoughts.

You will never be able to finish the business in your head. No matter how your mind tries to retell and spin the situation, you will keep hitting roadblocks. You will become physically and mentally drained. Think about the last time you spent a lot of time in your head trying to figure something out. How did you feel afterwards? Were you ready to conquer the world? Probably not. You might have even found it challenging to wash dishes, be present with your children, make a phone call, work on an assignment, or begin a work project.

The best way to deal with unfinished business is to finish it. If you have an unresolved issue with someone, try talking to him. If communication doesn't work, commit to taking care of your emotional needs so that the other person no longer has the power to influence your mood. You could vow to change the way you deal with the other person so that she will not have the opportunity to hurt you again. If you have an issue with a person who is emotionally or physically unavailable or deceased, practice letting go of the attachment to wanting an apology or validation of your feelings. Practice validating yourself. Self-validation might look like telling your-self: 'I feel what I feel, and that is ok. Nothing more, nothing less.'

During moments of intense feelings of agitation, it might be helpful to ask yourself the following questions:

- What internal gift could I give to my Self that does not blame or shame my Self or the other person?
- How can I own my internal baggage that is getting in the way of me letting go of the hold that others have on my life?

CONSIDER THE GIFT OF unconditional acceptance of your feelings at this moment. Make a commitment to your Self to act based upon your values and not your feelings.

Allow your feelings to be your feelings. They change fre-quently. Just allow them to flow through your body, and do not stop the feeling from taking its natural course. Mindful Acceptance encourages us to compassionately acknowledge the presence of our thoughts and be intentional and creative about continuing to engage with ourselves, others, and the world in productive and effective ways. The practice of Mind-ful Acceptance prevents us from getting lost in the stories that our thinking self creates by increasing our awareness of the stories, being intentional about where we choose to focus our attention, and utilizing self-compassion and creativity throughout the entire process.

For people who are particularly tormented by thoughts of being abandoned or rejected, it might be helpful to consider this thinking self to be an inner child. This inner child needs what most children need: unconditional compassion, patience, acceptance, and love. Many people have tried to bring peace to this inner child with positive thinking, participation in healthy relationships, and moderate exercising, which seem to help quiet her for a while, but never permanently.

Practice telling yourself: 'I feel what I feel, and that is ok. Nothing more, nothing less.'

We all know people who have tried to control this active and verbal inner child by abusing food, alcohol, or drugs. Even the more constructive strategies can be dangerous when used in excess. Relying solely on exercise to deal with feelings of anxiety might lead to an exercise addiction. Similarly, positive thinking may prevent someone from leaving an abusive relationship. We need to learn how to flexibly engage in productive and meaningful behaviors that best meet our needs in any given situation.

The limited world of *should*

WHEN YOU WERE YOUNG, did you fantasize about where you would be in life as you grew up? If so, have you reached all those milestones? Well done if you have! If you are like the many people who have not reached their milestones when expected, how are you dealing with this reality? Are you wasting time lamenting over how things *should* be, or are you rewriting your story based upon your current reality? You can't change your past, but you can influence your future by mastering how you behave Today, Now, in this Present Moment.

As long as you have breath, it's not too late to develop the habit of exiting the world of should and entering the reality of Now.

I'VE KNOWN MANY SUCCESSFUL LADIES who think they *should* have been married with children by age 35. When dating, these women often behave in ways that demonstrate that they are overzealous for a mate. The result is generally the opposite of what they want. They usually push potential partners away because of the undue pressure to commit. These women could minimize their suffering by being mindful of *should* statements that are coming to their minds and dictating their behaviors. When the *should* statement (that they *should* be married with children by now) is brought to their attention, they can become intentional about thinking *it would be nice if* I were married with children instead of I *should* be married with children. This practice can become a happiness habit that allows them to not take their thoughts so seriously and behave in ways that are conducive to them getting what they want out of their lives and relationships. As long as you have breath, it's not too late to develop the habit of exiting the world of *should* and entering the reality of Now.

As a form of emotional self-care, would you consider making it a habit to convert *should* statements to *it would be nice if* statements? Have you noticed how you feel when you say to yourself, 'I should have known better than to overcommit to that task?' It sounds punitive—as if something is wrong with you. Contrast the previous *should* statement with this statement: 'It would have been nice if I hadn't agreed to that task.' Do you notice the difference? The *it would be nice if* statement was less critical, demanding, and shaming. Sure, the *it would be nice if* statement is longer, but it feels better and allows wiggle room for healthy decisions.

Should is a problematic way of communicating with others. Would you consider a recent dialogue with someone where the conversation began fruitful and positive but eventually deteriorated? If so, the presence of should statements might have contributed to the detour of the conversation.

When you tell a person that she *should* know better, there is the implication that she is defective or something is wrong with her because she doesn't know something that everyone else knows. Now, the conversation will be about her character and not the issue at hand.

ALWAYS AND *NEVER* STATEMENTS can get in the way of healthy dialogues with the Self and others. Most behaviors do not occur *always*. They might occur sometimes and often. Be mindful of saying that a person *never* does something the way you want it. There is a high possibility that people will engage in specific behaviors at least once. Using *always* and *never* in conversations with others are quick ways to move away from the issue at hand, and move toward something that has nothing to do with why the conversation was started.

In the workplace, should, ought, must, always, and never statements can lead to resentment among employees. What if a manager tells you that you are *always* late? You would probably take offense to that because you are not *always* late. You are late sometimes, but not *always*.

Consider increasing the habit of replacing should, must, and ought with *it would be nice if* and always and never to sometimes and often. Notice the difference in how the conversation flows without the use of those character-attacking, shaming, and absolute words.

Labels that limit

If we hold labels too tightly, we could be limiting ourselves from reaching or exceeding our potential: 'I'm a procrastinator,' and 'I've always been like this.' This mindset will provide you with an excuse for not changing. This is the exact opposite of Mindful Acceptance and 'It is what it is.' Procrastination is a behavior. You can change a behavior.

Mel Robbins suggests that most people do not procrastinate because they are lazy, but because they are avoiding doing something stressful.

I've heard many people say, 'I procrastinate because I'm lazy.' Think about it. If you have a big project due, wouldn't it be overwhelming to think about such a daunting task? How do you prevent feeling overwhelmed? You don't think about the project, and you don't do it. Like many people, you wait until the 11th hour to tackle the project because you can't put it off any longer.

COLTON EXPLAINED THAT HE HAD an epiphany regarding why he procrastinated about doing things that are important, especially at work. He explained that if he started the project in advance, then he would forfeit having an excuse for not doing a good job. If he waited until the last minute to complete the project and it didn't turn out perfect, then he could justify it to himself by saying, 'It would have been perfect if I had more time.' This situation may seem odd, but it occurs more often than many people realize. This situation is common among people prone to thinking that they are a failure if a project isn't perfect. The solution to this concern is to be mindful of perfectionistic thoughts and be intentional about committing to thoughts and actions that move you closer to your goal. Let's consider being intentional in our thoughts, doing our best, and getting things done.

OUR MINDS WANT TO MAKE SENSE of our internal and external environments. When we can't understand our behavior, our minds ramp up by attempting to figure us out, label us, and put us in a cute little box. Not talking to new people because of the label, 'I'm shy,' is especially problematic if you deeply want to meet new people. I understand that you describe yourself as shy because of your fear of what other people might think of you. Thoughts and emotions do not prevent you from meeting new people unless you give them permission.

Suppose you want to increase your support system. How are you going to meet new people? I suggest that you can be shy and meet new people. In order to engage in social activities, you might have to let go of the label that you are shy. It might be helpful to be mindful of what you are internally experiencing. Practice describing your private behaviors, such as the thoughts that come up when you think about meeting people and the sensations that you feel in your body, such as a knot in your stomach or tightness in your chest.

Next, become intentional, self-compassionate, and creative about committing to the challenge of courageously acting based upon what's important to you, not based upon what your mind says or how you feel.

We all have unwelcome, intrusive thoughts

WE CAN'T ADDRESS OR COPE with thoughts that are outside our awareness. These thoughts are called *automatic thoughts* because they spontaneously occur. Many people who come to see me are overwhelmed with the concern that whatever they are thinking and feeling in the present moment will haunt them forever and destroy their lives. Thinking that something bad will last forever is called *catastrophizing*, which makes a situation worse than it is: a catastrophe.

'Don't make a mountain out of a molehill.'
— *Anonymous proverb*

ALLOW YOUR THOUGHTS AND EMOTIONS to just be what they are, without judgments and evaluations. We must realize that our true, observing self is vast and can contain and notice all thoughts and emotions. We don't have to react to every thought that comes to our minds.

Be intentional about telling yourself, 'It is what it is,' so that you can have the emotional energy to engage in meaningful behaviors. Internal fighting, evaluating, and trying to figure out what is going on in our head is emotionally and physically draining. If you are anxious about an upcoming situation and spend a lot of time dreading and replaying the possible negative outcomes, you will set yourself up to be at a disadvantage to the situation before you even enter it. We can be intentional about thinking thoughts that are positive, realistic, calming, and relaxing. We can be intentional about engaging in behaviors that are in the direction of what we want our life to be about.

Most of our thoughts are automatic, coming from our genetics, our past, and our experiences within the environment. Thoughts are harmful only if we create unhealthy stories about what they mean about us and believe them. It would be harmful to believe that you are an awful person because you had an unkind thought about a parent, partner, friend, or child. Disturbing thoughts like these may come and go. If you don't agree with a particular thought, don't make an agreement with it. Simply let it go and allow the thought to float away rather than giving it attention and allowing it to develop its own story.

You're fired!

THE BOOK OF PROVERBS SAYS, 'For as a man thinketh in his heart, so is he.' Some people have taken this to mean that every thought that has come to their mind is of their choosing and must be true. This simply is not the case. You can do yourself a big favor by being mindful of continuing to reclaim your Best Self by firing the thoughts that are not true to your chosen values. Practice saying to unhelpful thoughts: 'You're fired!'

As a way to deal with unhealthy thoughts, it might be helpful to include this mantra as part of your emotional self-care: 'I am not my thoughts.'

DON'T ALLOW FEAR-BASED, disempowering, critical, and judgmental thoughts to have a prominent place in your life. Notice them, but don't hire them to inform your behavior. Hire the positive, realistic, empowering, and motivating thoughts to inform your behavior.

Have thoughts ever come to your mind that were totally out of character and possibly somewhat wicked? If so, have you ever acted on these wicked thoughts? Probably not. Welcome to being human. When you practice firing thoughts that are not working for you, allowing emotions to flow through you, and behaving in non-people-pleasing ways, you will be truly free to fully indulge in all the wonders, vitality, love, and beauty of being alive and human.

Many of my clients can relate when I jokingly say, 'My mind has a mind of its own.' You are not your thoughts unless you agree with them and give them attention and energy. You are much more than your thoughts. If you acknowledge the presence of the thoughts, and choose not to give them energy, they will wax and wane, and eventually not have a significant impact on your well-being. As a way to deal with unhealthy thoughts, it might be helpful to include this mantra as part of your emotional self-care: 'I am not my thoughts.'

Help for unwanted thoughts

THE FIRST STEP toward dealing with intrusive or unwelcome thoughts is to bring them to our awareness by pausing, breathing, and noticing the messages that our minds are sending to us with gentleness, compassion, and honesty. In her book, *Radical Acceptance*, Tara Brach explains what she calls the Sacred Pause. She describes this pause as 'a suspension of activity, a time of temporary disengagement when we are no longer moving toward any goal.' I see this pause as taking a personal time-out, allowing a moment of reflection, or taking a step back to regroup. This pause will help you reassess and realign your Self with your goals and values as you decide how you want to relate to unwelcome thoughts, emotions, people, and the world.

The Sacred Pause can be used in many areas of our lives, particularly at work. Many of us have demanding jobs that are emotionally and physically exhausting. Even if you work in an office and sit at a desk, that is physically draining because sitting for long hours and looking at a computer screen can be taxing on your body. When we are physically drained, it often has a negative impact on our emotions. As a form of emotional self-care, consider pausing throughout the day and engaging in conscious breathing: breathe in, 'I relax my body,' and breathe out, 'I release the tension.' This will help you rejuvenate and refuel as you continue to deal with constant emails, fire drills, telephone calls, difficult people, and interpersonal drama.

It is not our thoughts that affect our situation and life outcome, but it is how we relate to our thoughts and our resulting behaviors that contribute to our goals and valued life direction.

THE EXAMINATION OF UNWANTED THOUGHTS might seem scary to tackle alone. A licensed therapist is a good place to start when it comes to exploring the intrusive thoughts that are outside your conscious awareness. A therapist can help you notice your thoughts so that you will be able to choose how to deal with them. You can choose to challenge and attempt to replace them with positive thoughts as traditional *cognitive-behavioral therapy* would suggest. A thought cannot be erased, but you can choose to fire it, by not believing it, thereby making it a 'non-factor' in your life.

You can choose to acknowledge and allow thoughts that you cannot change to come and go. Or, you can choose to be creative by picking and choosing among whatever skills might work for you. As you master your mind, you become the master of your Universe. Some *acceptance and commitment* therapists say when referring to the mind metaphorically, 'You have to put that puppy on a leash.'

It is not our thoughts that affect our situation and life outcome, but it is how we relate to our thoughts and our resulting behaviors that contribute to our goals and valued life direction. I encourage us all to be mindful of our current mindset, and if it is not working for us, let's be intentional, compassionate, and creative about changing what we can to engage fully in the world and live a life of joy, vitality, and meaning. If your mindset is problematic, adopt a new one and engage in behaviors aligned with your new mindset until it becomes habit.

It is what it is, so let it be

IF YOU ACKNOWLEDGE YOUR THOUGHTS and leave them alone, they will come and go like the clouds passing by, leaves flowing down a stream, or the many cars passing by in an urban city. Resistance to what we cannot change is the root of much of our suffering. As adults, we can change our current reality by changing jobs, partners, environments, and problematic behaviors. We cannot change our intrusive thoughts and natural emotions. We pine over what we want to happen, what we think we *should* be doing, and how we wish we would feel. We would do better in life if we spent less time languishing over what would've, could've, or should've happened in the past and more time making and creating the life we want to live, right Now.

I CANNOT CHANGE THAT MY MIND tells me that life is overwhelming when my children are acting out. My family currently resides in Charlotte, NC, and we do not get snow very often. My daughters had been begging for snow all winter. Then, the day arrived. It snowed. They were so excited when they awakened and discovered the neighborhood blanketed in newly fallen snow. We got out of bed early, bundled up, and went outside to play in the snow. Within minutes, shenanigans began. My 6-year-old wanted to shovel the driveway. Sounds like fun, right? Well, my 4-year-old didn't want her to shovel at all. I imagine she thought that her sister was trying to get rid of all the snow. Nevertheless, they spent precious time arguing. They weren't distracted by the beauty of the morning. While they fought, I wondered what it would be like to enjoy the crisp morning in peace and solitude. My mind told me that my girls should be on a reality show for ungrateful, spoiled, and bratty children. My mind didn't stop there. It continued to spew out 'what if's' about my life that included a quiet and calm external environment. I was becoming frustrated as I was beginning to get hooked by the words going through my head, *Why couldn't they just enjoy the darn snow?* Eventually, I noticed my mood shifting to despondency and I was becoming angry for being frustrated. I used my mood shift as an alert for to me snap out of it.

In this situation, had I taken my thoughts too seriously and became caught up in them, I might have gone down the rabbit hole of thinking that I am a bad parent for thinking certain thoughts. Instead, I became intentional about noticing the internal chatter and allowed the chatter to chat. It is what it is! When I stop, pause, and really listen to what my mind is saying, and take it lightly, I often find that my chatterbox has an interesting sense of humor. I laugh at my chatterbox, and we all know that laughter is good for the soul.

---

*Life will continually provide us with opportunities
to apply the principle 'it is what it is.'*

MINDFUL ACCEPTANCE TEACHES US to be mindful, intentional, compassionate, and creative about changing things that are within our control, such as our own behavior and our own personal reality. Mindful Acceptance does not employ the concept of 'it is what it is' in situations that we can change, such as leaving an abusive partner, changing jobs, or minimizing contact with toxic family. We do not say, 'It is what it is,' about giving up on our goals and what matters most to us because we can alter our behavior to move toward our goals and values.

Life will continually provide us with opportunities to apply the principle 'it is what it is.' Uncomfortable emotions become intensified when we hope that we are not feeling and thinking 'what is,' which is what we are currently thinking and feeling. Gentleness with what we are experiencing in the present moment could be good for our soul.

NOT TOO LONG AGO, MY FRIEND CLAIRE became frustrated with her husband because he would not schedule a dentist appointment. For an entire week, Claire asked whether he had made the appointment. Claire was beginning to maneuver out of her lane as a supportive wife and swerve into the lane of a controlling mother. She was thinking that if he didn't get his cavities taken care of, he could be at risk for gum disease, which is a cause of heart disease. She was beginning to experience what is called *anticipatory anxiety,* which is anxiety about something that may not happen in the future.

The next time she thought about his dentist appointment, she chose a different route. She began to practice what she learned from her talks with me. She became mindful and increased her awareness that it was her husband's dental hygiene that was being compromised, not her own. She intentionally thought to herself, 'Although we became one in matrimony, we are still separate entities that make up the whole. We are a yin yang, a beautiful whole. He is entitled to handle his dental hygiene however he likes.' She acknowledged to herself that his dental hygiene was his responsibility, not hers.

Claire increased self-compassion for her frustration; she was patient with herself. She became creative in generating compassion for herself and for him. She thought to herself that apparently somewhere in his life he didn't get the memo about the importance of dental hygiene. She didn't tell him this thought. She just thought this to herself, which made her smile and ease the internal frustration. The next time she reminded him about the dentist, Claire was intentional about ending the conversation, 'Ok, if you say so, it's *your* mouth.' I was very proud of Claire in her ability to behave intentionally and go on about her day without ruminating about this situation. She refused to remain frustrated; instead, she committed to experiencing the present moments of her day with a relaxed, calm, and collected posture.

OUR RELATIONSHIPS WITH FAMILY MEMBERS will provide ample opportunity for practicing the disciplines of Mindful Acceptance. Kim's grandmother may comment on her weight each time she sees her. Even if it's only been a few days since they've seen each other, she greets her granddaughter with: 'Kim, have you gained weight?' Kim had just seen her last week. She could not have gained noticeable weight in just a few days! Kim's immediate reaction was frustration, which was out of her control. What can Kim do? Behaviors, not automatic thoughts and emotions, are within Kim's control. Does she become preoccupied with whether she *should* have eaten cake last week? Does she get snippy with the old lady? Or does she say to herself, 'It is what it is. I can't control what my grandmother says.'

The first thing to remember about situations like this one is that it might not be a comment intended to cause harm. Kim's grandmother may have simply forgotten how to start a conversation.

Consider making it a habit of finding ways to not personalize situations. Become intentional and creative about finding the humor in situations that don't have to be so serious. Kim discovered how to internally laugh at the idea that her old granny had lost the ability to politely start a conversation.

Best Self in Action: Unwanted thoughts

YOUR MIND IS ALWAYS GOING AT FULL SPEED. It is up to you to slow it down and notice the shenanigans that are going on. We have to be mindful that we are not our thoughts and be intentional about creating thoughts that will help move us towards our goals. Consider what thoughts in your head work for you and what thoughts and beliefs no longer work for you. Allow the thoughts that work for you to inform your behavior.

Remember that your Best Self isn't lived in your head. It is experienced in the world. Commit every day to increasing thoughts that will contribute to living as your Best Self.

MIND PAIN

THE ROMAN MORALIST PUBLILIUS SYRUS once said, 'The pain of the mind is worse than the pain of the body.' You might be suffering in silence because of the fear of sharing your mind pain with other people. In the past, you might have tried to tell someone how you felt about a particular matter, and they might have invalidated you by saying that you shouldn't feel that way or that's not how it happened. This happens often when adult children attempt to discuss their childhood with their parents. If the adult child's story is not flattering of the parent, the parent will be unable to validate the adult child because it is often too painful for the parent. The situation becomes about the parent and not the adult child trying to share her truth. You might have stopped trusting your own emotions, learned to keep your emotional pain to yourself, and suffered in silence.

Emotional pain is inevitable, temporary, and universal to the human experience.

IT IS TRUE, AND MAYBE UNFAIR, that people receive more support and assistance when they are suffering physically, but not so much when they are suffering emotionally. That is not an excuse to suffer in silence. Blaming others for not noticing and caring for your emotional needs is not going to be helpful.

Be creative about finding a supportive person with whom to share your story. Don't limit yourself to the support from family. The support might come from where you least expect it. Open your mind to the many avenues from where support might come: a boss, mentor, or therapist. Ask for what you need. Own what is getting in the way of your success. Stop defending stories that are not working for you. Let them go, if necessary.

The intensity of psychological pain in someone's life begins in the mind, just as happiness, sorrow, peace, and resistance. The way that one relates to pain will determine its impact. Painful situations don't have to be miserable. Misery and suffering are optional. We have the power to choose to experience psychological pain without making the bad situation worse.

Emotional pain is inevitable, temporary, and universal to the human experience. Each one of us has at least one thing in common: we will all experience psychological pain at some point. Many of us want to appear strong and put together, but we can't escape pain. The irony is that it takes greater strength and courage to reveal our pain to others than it does to hold on to it and act as if it doesn't exist. As we decide how we want to cope with pain, we need to be mindful that the feeling of isolation felt from not sharing our story often places us at risk of transforming the inevitable and normal pain into long-term suffering and misery.

The mind trap of pain

MOST PEOPLE DO NOT CHOOSE to feel miserable. Nevertheless, many people slip into a mind trap of pain by perceiving it as enduring and long lasting and will do whatever it takes in an attempt to get rid of it. The reality is that psychological pain, like other emotions, is short-term and will change just as the weather does throughout the day. The emotion of pain is simply 'energy in motion.' Allow this energy to flow through you without justifying or explaining it. When we judge our emotions, we prevent the emotion from naturally flowing through us, which makes us feel stuck. We often ask ourselves, 'What's wrong with me for feeling this way?' Nothing is wrong with you. You are entitled to feel whatever you are feeling in this moment. Even if you don't understand or agree with the feeling, don't stop it from flowing. Just allow it to travel through your body.

Emotions are transient. If we practice intentional patience and conscious breathing, the emotion will eventually change. Just give it a moment. Emotions do not require a storyline. When you feel emotions rumble or move within you, an attempt to name the emotion is helpful: 'I'm feeling hurt.' Then, I suggest you have intentional coping statements available to assist you. Consider saying to yourself: 'I'm entitled to feel what I feel,' and 'It is what it is, so I'm going to let it be.'

If you do not have coping statements memorized, it might be helpful to create coping cards. Coping cards are reminders to help you self-soothe. These can be created with index cards and a metal ring. Write coping statements on the index cards, punch holes in the cards, and attach them to the metal ring. Remember to keep them nearby. Many women put them in their purses, while men just keep them in their pockets. Recite them often, and they will eventually commit to memory. People who believe in the power of coping statements are good at self-soothing and are likely to have access to their Best Self.

Don't make a bad situation worse

BECOME AWARE OF THE MIND TRAP OF PAIN. If you think that you must get rid of pain immediately so that it won't last forever, break the cycle by increasing your awareness of how it works. The next time that you experience psychological pain, would you consider being intentional about reminding yourself that pain is temporary and that the God of your understanding or the Universe will not give you more than you can bear?

'Wisdom is nothing more than healed pain.'
— Robert Gary Lee

ALL OF US WILL SUFFER FROM broken relationships, deaths of loved ones, or financial loss. There is no way to sugar coat this situation. There will be pain for all of us, and lots of it! Remember, pain will eventually decrease in intensity if we don't make it worse. A painful situation, such as a partner cheating, could be made worse by driving to a bar, drinking into a stupor, and driving home. Some people blame their unhealthy responses on other people's behaviors, such as to their partner's unfaithfulness. No, our partner does not make us engage in unwise decisions. Getting caught up in emotions and thoughts leads to poor decisions.

We have to learn how to make wise decisions even when we are in emotional pain. Mindful Acceptance is available to help you deal with your life situation and take responsibility for caring for your adult needs. I encourage you to become aware of what you are thinking and how you are feeling in a painful situation, allow yourself to experience normal pain and pain reactions without judgment, and compassionately make intentional and wise decisions that have your best long-term interest in mind.

If we can learn to wait out an uncomfortable situation without making a 'bad situation worse,' we could reap the benefits of growth, resiliency, and life purpose. People who have endured unthinkable circumstances have claimed that their suffering made them stronger. These people are not superhuman: they simply accepted the reality of their situation and learned how to survive without making things worse. These people were resilient. They did not see setbacks as failures, but as growth opportunities.

Learning to feel

WE CAN FIND PURPOSE when we look at our psychological pain with curiosity and openness instead of resistance and avoidance. Pain is something that we all will face in life; we cannot control or avoid it. What we can do is become aware of problematic behaviors that are based on feelings. Avoiding people or situations and engaging in unhealthy behaviors to prevent anxiety or sadness gives us the illusion of control. We are simply being distracted from our intrusive thoughts and uncomfortable emotions, not eradicating them. Distraction isn't necessarily a bad thing. Certainly, it can be useful if it helps us engage in purposeful and worthwhile behavior. Yet, after the distraction has ended, the thoughts and emotions may resurface. Then, the cycle begins again.

Many people feel worse because they were unable to make specific thoughts and emotions go away permanently. A solution is to practice feeling our feelings instead of engaging in behaviors to avoid feeling certain emotions. An intentional self-statement to help you feel your feelings might be, 'I'm entitled to feel however I feel at this moment.' Many ACT therapists say that instead of helping clients to *feel* good, we need to help clients *learn* to feel.

CASEY'S SENSE OF SELF WAS DERIVED from being a wife and mother. She faced a difficult transition when her children moved out of the house. Given that Casey no longer had the responsibilities of dealing with the children's busy schedule, she realized that she and her husband had little in common. When he was home, he was either in another room or on his cell phone. They rarely conversed. Casey felt like the marriage was sucking the life out of her, but for 25 years that is all she had known.

One dreary day, things changed for Casey. Her husband said he wasn't happy and wanted a divorce. Casey begged him to stay and said she would do whatever he wanted to make the relationship better. Her spouse adamantly refused the gestures and said that he had moved on with a new lover. Casey was torn on so many levels. She cried, and cried, and cried. She went through a range of emotions from anger to sadness to denial to bargaining and after much suffering, acceptance. Before she could move on with her life, she had to make peace with her feelings. She had to learn how to feel her emotions without being controlled by them.

Casey allowed the pain of divorce to transform into an opportunity for self-exploration.

PSYCHOLOGICAL PAIN OFTEN OCCURS when external changes occur in our life such as job layoffs, relationship break-ups, and relocations. In *Managing Transitions: Making the Most of Change*, William Bridges argues that external changes often trigger people to make a transition, which is an internal acceptance of the end of some phase of life and the beginning of another. Bridges states, 'transition always starts with an ending. To become something else, you have to stop being what you are now; to start doing things a new way, you have to end the way you are doing them now; and to develop a new attitude or outlook, you have to let go of the old.'

Casey allowed herself to experience guilt and shame by re-framing how she perceived the emotions. She began to see them as normal emotions to her life transition. She was able to look at what her emotions were telling her that she needed in order to move to the next chapter in her life. Once Casey had accepted her loss, she decided to get to know herself and do some things she had neglected because of her family and husband.

Casey hadn't traveled because her husband did not like to fly. Casey decided to tour the world, read self-help books, and reconnect with friendships that she had allowed to fall by the wayside. Casey allowed the pain of divorce to transform into an opportunity for self-exploration. Had she believed the stories that her mind told her, that she was worthless because she no longer had the same role in her family as a loving wife and mother, her pain would have taken her down a very dark path. Well, she did go down a dark path. However, she did not stay there. The dark path awakened a part of her that she did not know existed. Thankfully, Casey did not make her situation worse by allowing her pain to consume her. Instead, she allowed the pain to be what it was and began a new chapter in her life.

Best Self in Action: Coping with emotional pain

DON'T SUFFER SILENTLY because of emotional mind pain. Some situations are painful, but they don't have to be traumatic. Our pain is intensified by our appraisal. The pain could simply be painful. Or, depending on how we evaluate the situation that triggered the pain, the pain could be transformed into misery.

Be mindful that you control the intensity of the pain that you experience from external situations. Throughout the day, practice noticing when you become emotionally stuck in a painful area. Notice the pain and actively allow it to flow without positively or negatively appraising it. Practice saying, 'It is what it is.'

EMOTIONS ARE OVER-RATED

T HERE'S NO SUCH THING AS A GOOD EXCUSE. We can't use emotions as an excuse for not doing what we want to do in life. Emotions do not prevent us from behaving a certain way or make us behave another way. As the American psychologist, William James, suggested, 'I don't sing because I'm happy. I'm happy because I sing.' James postulated that emotions occur after behavior, not the other way around. Common situations where people blame emotions for not fully engaging and enjoying life include:

- Camryn wanted to lose weight, but she didn't go to the gym today because she felt tired.
- Andy really wanted to meet new people, but he didn't make it to the after-work event because he felt nervous.

- Jason wanted to attend graduate school, but he didn't take the GRE because he felt anxious.

YOUR MIND CAN CREATE AN ENTIRE STORY full of reasons why you can't have the life that you deserve. Your mind will creatively find a way to complete the sentence and try to hook you with one of its fanciful stories. Feeling tired, nervous, or inadequate are excuses, not reasons for behavior.

All of us have the ability to behave based on our values and not our ever-changing emotions. If you do not believe me, think about a time when you felt horrible and didn't want to do something. However, the behavior was meaningful to you and you did it anyway. This is evidence that your emotions do not control your behaviors. We need to be intentional about making statements using *and* instead of *but* when we are making decisions about our behavior. For instance:

- Camryn wants to lose weight. She feels tired, *and* she goes to the gym today.
- Andy really wants to meet new people. He feels nervous, *and* he attends the after-work event.
- Jason wants to attend graduate school. He feels anxious, *and* he takes the GRE.

AN EMOTION IS JUST AN EMOTION. As a form of emotional self-care, we need to accept that no emotion in and of itself is negative. Emotions can become problematic, exaggerated, and intensified when our minds begin to create irrational and compelling stories instead of simply allowing them *to be*. Emotions have evolved for our survival.

Our perceived negative emotions of worry, sadness, and frustration have always been with us, and at one time were considered our ally in the fight for survival. They just have a bad rap and are often seen as negative. These emotions help alert us to what is going on inside, outside, and around us.

- *Worry* alerts us to possible danger.
- *Sadness* gets us in touch with our soft and compassionate side.
- *Frustration* informs us that we may be at risk of getting hurt.

ALL EMOTIONS WORK TOGETHER to help us live a full and meaningful life. Things go awry when we begin to resist certain aspects of life, such as thinking that we aren't *supposed* to feel or think a certain way.

Recently, my client, Helen, dejectedly told me that she hates herself for feeling jealous of other people in her graduate program. She explained that she wants to feel happy for her peers, but she couldn't move past her own feelings. Helen wasted a lot of time feeling sorry for herself for not being where she wants to be in her program and for feeling jealous of her colleagues. Helen would do herself some good to become intentional about refocusing her attention from blame and comparison to setting goals and getting things done.

The most successful people in the world take ownership of their behavior and act in ways that are aligned with their values.

MANY PEOPLE ENGAGE in unhelpful behaviors or avoid helpful behaviors in an attempt to prevent feeling certain emotions such as loneliness, rejection, vulnerability, sadness, or anxiety. None of these emotions are particularly negative. They are present in all of us, but we each have unique histories, temperaments, and genetics that contribute to the way we evaluate emotions. It is our evaluation of emotions that gets us stuck and overwhelmed. Mindful Acceptance helps us to become aware of the excuses that we use to justify behavior. We cannot experience personal growth and transformation until we stop blaming and making excuses for our behavior. The most successful people in the world take ownership of their behavior and act in ways that are aligned with their values.

SUSANNA LOVES to be in committed relationships. She typically remains in a relationship past its termination date and tolerates inappropriate behavior. Susanna justifies her behavior by saying that she doesn't like the feeling of being alone. Susanna no longer knows who she is, what she wants, or what she values because she has acquired a habit of pleasing and accommodating others in an attempt to avoid loneliness. Simply put, Susanna has lost herself in other people.

Jacob plays it safe in life. For the most part, he does exactly what people expect. He graduated from high school, then college, and eventually landed a decent paying job at a local bank. Jacob is not a risk taker, doesn't like being told no, and he despises failure. Jacob hasn't been in many relationships because he fears rejection. Jacob has allowed his fear of rejection to prevent him from applying to upper level job positions. Jacob's mindset is that he is waiting to explore life outside his comfort zone when he no longer cares about being rejected.

Jayden is always juggling two or three women at the same time. Often, women are unaware that he is unfaithful. Growing up, he witnessed his mother being hurt by different men, and he vowed to never put himself in that type of situation. Jayden justifies his lack of commitment by claiming that he just hasn't found the right mate. Jayden is unknowingly protecting himself from getting hurt.

Lucy feels sad when her mind torments her about the *bad* things that she has done in the past. She uses her sadness as an excuse for problematic behavior. When sad, Lucy chain-smokes between cigarettes and marijuana until she passes out. She has unprotected sex with several different guys, which makes her feel desirable. The good feeling is short-lived. Lucy feels worse after the high wears off. Ironically, Lucy's risky behavior feeds her feelings of sadness, and she feels worse about herself because of the high-risk behavior. Lucy is constantly on the lookout for anything or anyone who can take the sadness away, even momentarily.

Donald is terrified of any type of travel—except for by car. He watches a lot of news and says that the world is not safe. Donald experiences extreme anxiety, such as tightness in his chest, knots in his throat, and dry mouth whenever his wife pressures him to travel by air, train, or boat. He uses his anxiety to justify why he is not traveling with his family. Donald has family in Jamaica that he refuses to visit because of his anxiety. His immediate family has gone on family trips without him. Donald and his wife argue often because he wants to drive to places that would take 12 or more hours to reach by car, but less than three hours by plane. Donald's behaviors are limited by his anxiety. He says that once he gets rid of his anxiety, then, he will travel and reconnect with his family.

In all the above scenarios, individuals have made excuses and allowed their emotions to dictate their behavior in crucial situations. Susanna doesn't allow herself to be without a romantic partner long enough to get to know herself. Jacob shies away from challenging situations. Jayden avoids being in a committed relationship. Lucy engages in risky behavior, and Donald surrenders to his anxiety.

One suggestion for these individuals is to begin to bring to their awareness the impact that behaving based on emotions and excuses has had on their life, especially if it has prevented them from reaching success in any life domain. I would suggest that they consider what they want most out of their life. Do they want to continue to cater to and feed the emotion that is holding them back, or do they want to experience the vastness of life? What do they value? What are their goals?

People often say, 'I don't know when to trust my emotions, so how do I know how to behave?' My response is to be intentional about asking yourself about a particular behavior:

- What is the purpose of this behavior?
- Will this behavior help me get what I want out of life?
- Is this behavior based upon desiring a particular feeling or trying to get rid of a feeling?

The purpose of worry

THOUSANDS OF YEARS AGO, if we were living in the wild, it made sense for us to worry about bears and other animals. Thankfully, for most of us, bears and wild animals are no longer a major concern.

If you have an upcoming exam for advancement in your career, you need a little worry to encourage you to study. If you didn't worry, maybe you wouldn't take the exam seriously enough to study. It is all about how you relate to the worry. If you allow the worry to prevent you from studying, then that's when worry becomes problematic. However, you can choose to transform the jittery energy of worry into the needed physical energy to study. You can transform anxiety into physical energy by being intentional about reminding yourself of why you are studying for your exam and the importance of it to the advancement of your career. This information can be used to guide your behavior.

We can take a kind and gentle stance toward our sadness, loneliness, and anxiety. What if we could perceive our private experiences as a newborn child who needs to be held tenderly? Would you get mad at an infant for crying? The reality of it is that thoughts and emotions, both positive and negative, are not going anywhere. They will always be with us as our shadow, friend, or whatever we choose to call them. A true awareness and acceptance of this concept are the first steps toward changing our relationship with ourselves, enjoying the fruits of our labor, and maximizing the time that we have in this lifetime.

From feeling better to doing better

THE ATTEMPT TO CONTROL what you cannot change could be keeping you from doing better, and everyone wants to do better.

You may say that you want to *feel* better. Who doesn't? Feeling better doesn't necessarily get you what you want in life. Most people don't want to feel better for the sake of feeling better. Most people think they want to feel better so they can accomplish some goal. I have heard many people say that if they felt better, they would be more social, go on a job interview, connect with others, and be more productive. The irony of this situation is that feeling better doesn't necessarily increase positive behaviors. However, increasing meaningful and positive behaviors often does make people feel better. You might want to make it a habit to refocus your goals from *feeling* better to *doing* better, which in turn, often makes you feel better.

Don't take my word for it. Look at your experience and determine if you felt better after engaging in productive and positive behaviors.

Willingness isn't everything, but it helps.

WHAT IF YOU CAN'T MAKE YOURSELF do something that you know you need to do when you don't feel like it? Motivation to engage in positive behaviors, such as exercising, completing projects, and cleaning up, will not be present when you are tired, sad, depressed, anxious, bored, or overwhelmed. Don't wait on a feeling of motivation before doing something that you know is important.

I have two suggestions to combat *not feeling* like doing something meaningful. First, I suggest focusing on why doing a task is important to you and allowing the value of the task to give you the extra boost. Second, I suggest increasing your willingness skills. Willingness is a mindset of saying *Yes,* without conditions, to the Universe and to what is in your best interest. Are you willing to do what you need to do to live as your Best Self? The answer is simply yes or no. Willingness isn't everything, but it helps.

MOST OF US DON'T NEED more information about what we need to do in order to live successful lives. We need implementation skills. Mel Robbins, in the *5 Second Rule,* encourages us to say 5, 4, 3, 2, 1, and then engage in the important task as a way to encourage productive behavior. She suggests that visualizing a productive behavior and committing to doing that behavior at the end of a 5-second backward countdown prevents our mind from talking us out of doing the task. Visualization is encouraged because studies have shown that successful athletes and performers are often trained to visualize themselves successfully engaging in the behavior that they want to achieve. Other alternatives to the 5 Second Rule after first committing to a task, then visualizing yourself in the productive task include motivating self-talk such as, 'The Time is Now, Go!' and Nike's 'Just Do It.' You can envision the Swoosh sign with the Nike 'Just Do It' affirmation. The purpose of these skills is to disrupt the rationalizing and justifying self-talk of the thinking self that gets in the way of us doing what matters.

Our minds have an incessant access to excuses to prevent us from doing what we know we need to do. We are not going to be motivated to engage in certain behaviors. Try not to waste time exploring why you don't want to do something that you know is important. Use that time and energy to do what it is that you know needs to be done. The practice of these 'do it anyway' skills that disrupts our minds from getting in the way of our happiness will become a habit if we are intentional about practice. As a caution, 'do it anyway' skills are encouraged to be applied to valued behavior, not overexertion, impulsivity, or irrational behavior.

Best Self in Action: From feeling to doing

THE SAME WAY THAT WE ARE TOO TRUSTING of our thoughts, we are often too trusting of our emotions. Many people allow their emotions to prevent them from living their dreams because they don't *feel* a particular way. In the case where it is in our best interest to take action, but we don't feel like it, we need to practice acting based on our values, not our feelings. Embrace your Best Self and be mindful that feelings cannot always be trusted and they don't dictate our behaviors. Our behaviors inform our emotions. Practice surfing your emotions throughout the day by noticing them as they change throughout the day and riding them like a wave without trying to push them away or make them stay.

THE KEY TO LASTING HAPPINESS

THE AWARENESS OF WHAT HAPPINESS IS will help us practice Mindful Acceptance. The myths of happiness are abundant and sensationalized by the media. We are constantly told that happiness is our natural, resting state. Nothing could be further from the truth. Happiness is by design, not by default. Happiness is a lifestyle, a way of being. Pleasure, which is often mistaken for happiness, is found in external things. Happiness is cultivated from within and is not contingent upon others, situations, or things.

'Happiness depends upon ourselves.'
— Aristotle

OVER 2,000 YEARS AGO, Aristotle wrote that happiness comes from living a life full of purpose and in accordance with our virtues such as justice and courage. These virtues have nothing to do with wealth or outside circumstances and everything to do with how we behave. If we live a life in which we are doing our best, contributing to our society, and connecting with our spiritual world, then, according to Aristotle, we will experience happiness.

Aristotle believed that happiness is something that you can't say you've achieved until the end of your life and the sum of your behaviors has been totaled. I believe that we can experience happiness in the here and now as an active and value-driven way of living, not an end result. Happiness is a path that one chooses. My happiness path includes habits of emotional self-care such as approaching life with Mindful Acceptance, reframing of situations, noticing the stream of thoughts that go through my mind without engaging with them, breathing consciously, smiling often, and delaying emotional gratification in the moment.

WE ALL WANT WHAT WE WANT when we want it. However, a sign of psychological growth and maturity is the ability to delay emotional gratification. Delaying emotional gratification is a skill for lasting happiness. If your default behavior is to be confrontational and strong-willed, you might not feel at ease until you have confronted and engaged the situation. Timing is everything, and not every situation needs to be addressed and confronted when your mind says so. Delaying emotional gratification means we are aware of our default behaviors and intentional about doing what is best given the situation at hand.

The practice of happiness *is* happiness. Happiness is being aware that positive emotions are transient. If happiness were only based upon circumstances, then you would always be in an emotional state of flux vacillating between different shades of pleasure and pain. This emotional state is a set-up for always searching for the next big event to occur and swing the pendulum back to pleasure.

Everything about our society tells us that we *should* be happy, and if we are unhappy, something must be wrong with us. Most of us strive for future happiness. I will be happy when:

- I receive a promotion at my job.
- I marry the perfect partner.
- I step on the scale and notice that I am down 5 pounds.

- My Instagram picture receives over 1,000 likes and no dislikes.
- I relocate and start a new life.

MANY PEOPLE experience positive changes in their lives and are still searching for happiness. Privileged people often feel the saddest because they can't find an easy excuse or justification for their unhappiness. They say to themselves, 'It's understandable why people living in poverty would be sad, but I have everything, yet I feel like I have nothing.' 'What's wrong with me?' is the question that often leads people down the lonely, dark road of self-evaluating and self-judging.

In her 2007 book, *The How of Happiness*, Sonja Lyubomirsky concluded from her research that approximately 50% of happiness is determined by our genes and 10% by our life circumstance, but 40% depends on our daily internal and external activities. Even if an individual has a natural disposition toward happiness, at some points in time, as a normal individual, she may experience mood states of sadness, fear, and anxiety. This would imply that the reverse is true as well. If an individual has a seemingly natural disposition towards negativity, at some points in time, this individual may experience mood states of happiness, which could be increased and cultivated through intentional happiness habits.

What is happiness, really?

THERE ARE MANY DEFINITIONS FOR IT, but I prefer Russ Harris's suggestion that happiness is the result of 'living a rich, full and meaningful life.' Sonja Lyubomirsky's insight is useful as well: 'an experience of joy, contentment, or positive well-being, combined with a sense that one's life is good, meaningful, and worthwhile.' The good thing about these popular definitions is that happiness appears to be under our control. Lyubomirksy and Harris's definitions imply that if you are doing something meaningful in your life, then you are experiencing happiness.

I suggest that you might just not know that you are experiencing happiness because of what others have tried to tell you and the messages that are displayed in the media about the meaning of happiness. A mental reframe of what happiness means to you might help you notice that you already possess the ingredients for happiness and the search can be over. Happiness could be Now if you are willing to look within and let go of searching for happiness outside yourself. I encourage you to look beyond what you have been told about happiness, examine your experience, and begin your journey of happiness today. The journey of happiness begins with developing and engaging in happiness habits, such as approaching life with Mindful Acceptance and other habits of emotional self-care.

Happiness could be Now if you are willing to look within and let go of searching for happiness outside yourself.

WHAT MAKES US UNIQUELY HUMAN is our ability to think, plan, and choose. According to Lyubomirsky, at least 40% of happiness is a mental state and a personal choice. It is a state of being where one could choose to give energy to positive and realistic thoughts, feelings, and behaviors, or irrational, negative, and self-sabotaging thoughts, feelings, and behaviors. I choose to give attention to positive and realistic thoughts, feelings, and behaviors.

I am intentional about including realistic with positive thoughts because many people think in 'black and white' terms, 'I must pay attention and give full credence to all positive thoughts and completely ignore any negative thoughts.' There is as much threat to our happiness of getting caught up in positive thinking about every situation as it is to negative thinking about every situation. Mindful Acceptance encourages a relatively balanced, positive, yet realistic mindset of navigating our lives. We are encouraged to take all thoughts lightly and look at our real, lived experience to help guide us on our happiness journey.

People who choose to make positive and realistic thoughts and behaviors a habit appear to handle unpleasant events with grace. When unpleasant events occur, which they will, the person who chooses a positive and realistic outlook will experience the sad, anxious, or fearful emotions appropriate to the situation. Nothing more, nothing less. The emotion doesn't have to be good or bad. It is what it is: an ever-changing, temporary, ephemeral energy.

Approaching life with positive and realistic thoughts will allow you to experience sadness without depression, anger without infuriation, and anxiety without chronic worry. Positive and realistic thinking and behaviors will not get rid of negative and irrational thoughts, but they can help give you the necessary breathing room, emotional space, and courage to do the things that matter. It is much easier to make reasonable and rational decisions before stories have been created about why you feel a certain way. These stories, which are not fact-based, often escalate our emotions from '0 to 100,' really quick.

BE MINDFUL OF NOT LABELING YOURSELF. Practice labeling the behavior or emotion, not yourself. Your mind might tell you that you are an unhappy person because you are feeling sad. Acknowledge this thought without becoming one with it. Be intentional about saying to yourself, 'In this moment, I am experiencing sadness.' This statement doesn't imply that you *are* a happy or sad person, but it clearly states what you are experiencing in this moment. This statement can be practiced with experiencing happiness: 'In this moment, I am experiencing happiness.' We don't want to get too caught up in the feelings of happiness, either, because they will change. The lingering and longing for something to return or change will lead to suffering. Let's enjoy whatever the present moment has for us.

Freedom from psychological bondage

HAPPINESS AND SUCCESS IN ALL DOMAINS OF LIFE are achievable when we are free from mental knots, psychological triggers, internal sensitivities, and hot buttons. These energy-filled psychological roadblocks within us, which Buddhists call 'internal formations,' keep us bound and restricted to certain patterns of behaviors, such as being easily agitated, internally moved, and psychologically disturbed. It doesn't matter what word you use to describe these internal blocks; they all refer to the uncomfortable movement of energy inside us that alerts us to something deeper. It doesn't have to be a bad thing to which we are being alerted. It is just a thing to encourage us to increase our awareness of what is going on inside our physical and psychological bodies.

Your center is the mental place where you visit for comfort and peace.

HOW DO YOU KNOW if you have internal sensitivities? If you look at your life history, you will notice certain psychological areas in which you have consistently become stuck, angered, irritated, or annoyed. Given that emotions are energies, most often, you will notice an internal change in your body when you are triggered. I call this internal change an emotional rumble. Why do you think people say that someone pushed their buttons? They are talking about their psychological buttons that other people cannot see but that have been formed at some point in their lives.

Consider the last time that something or somebody really rubbed you the wrong way. See if you can remember how you felt inside. How and where did your emotions rumble in your body? I often feel a knot in my stomach to alert me that I might have a psychological trigger that has just been activated. Once you notice where in your body you feel the energy getting stuck on a knot, ask yourself, 'What is this feeling about that has nothing to do with another person or situation and what about me and my life makes me susceptible to be activated by this person or situation?' Provide loads of compassion to this area and allow the compassion to ground you and help you find your center. Your center is the mental place where you visit for comfort and peace. This type of compassionate introspection will help you untie the specific mental knot and no longer be activated and aroused about particular subjects and situations. You will be free to live your life without concern about being triggered. There is no need to avoid certain people, places, or things, or limit your behaviors in hopes of protecting your sensitivities.

The foundation for these internal formations is often formed when we are young. These formations may develop when we experience physical or emotional trauma or consistently receive certain messages about ourselves, others, and the world. Some fortunate children are taught how to prevent mental knots and mitigate triggers by being exposed to coping statements, positive affirmations, or wisdom teachings. We all have the mental landscape for knots to form by the mere fact that we are humans and we have the language to misconstrue or misevaluate innocent situations.

Once we develop the capacity to evaluate and judge, the foundation for mental knots is laid. It then becomes easy for knots to form and become entangled. The more entangled the knots, the more difficult to notice the knots and the more difficult to untie them. Because of these knots, we are unable to behave outside our comfort zone, stretch ourselves, and lean in to uncomfortable emotions when the situations call for such behaviors.

Mental knots are sensitivities within us that are easily agitated.

PEOPLE WHO ARE EASILY ANGERED often have mental knots that have not been untied. People filled with mental knots are often unaware of what triggers their agitation and find it difficult to not personalize external events. If you are unsure of whether you are plagued with internal knots, take an inventory of your relationship with your Self, others, and the world. If you notice difficulties, this is an indication that you might have unresolved issues or mental knots.

It is your responsibility to untie your mental knots and take ownership of your happiness. It is nice when we have people in our life who are willing to help us untie our mental knots, but it is still our responsibility to manage our emotional wellness.

If you are angry, don't blame others for your anger. It is not the world's responsibility to figure out what bothers you. What bothers one person may not bother another person. There is no way for one person to know everything that bothers everybody. In order to preserve your peace and happiness, it may be helpful to work on untying your knots so that you can engage in and with the world harmoniously.

The solution to untying mental knots lies in our ability to practice self-compassion. Self-compassion allows us to look within ourselves with a non-judgmental and non-evaluative posture about beliefs that are no longer serving us. Self-compassion encourages us to employ the same non-judgmental and non-evaluative stance towards things that happen to and around us that are not clearly understood. The misunderstanding of how other people work often contributes to mental knots being formed.

Our minds want to make sense of our world. The mind will create stories to make sense of ambiguous situations. Often times, the stories that are created are irrational and negative, but they seem to make sense to our minds at the time of creation. The negative story seems better than no story at all. Let go of the stories, and let go of the knots.

The beauty of minimizing our mental knots is that we are able to allow our emotions to flow through us without being stuck. If someone does something and our automatic reaction of anger occurs, the energy of anger can easily flow through us without becoming stuck and entangled in a knot.

Emotions are 'energy in motion.' Energy flows best when there is not an obstruction. By untying our mental knots, we are removing obstructions and allowing our emotions to easily come and go and change and flow. In order to prevent mental knots from forming, we need to make it a habit of being intentional about looking at ourselves, others, relationships, and the world with curiosity, awe, and intrigue. We need to be intentional about untying mental knots and preventing the formation of new ones. The practice of untying mental knots is a habit of happiness.

Lasting happiness

HAPPINESS IS A LIFESTYLE OF ACTIVELY ENGAGING in thoughts and behaviors that contribute to one's overall well-being. You can experience overwhelming happiness just from waking up in the morning and taking a deep breath. Nothing externally pleasurable or positive needs to occur to experience happiness.

I wake up grateful to experience a new day with my family. You may ask me if I am still happy after my 7-year-old daughter has just sassed me. No, I am not happy with her behavior, but yes, I still experience an overwhelming feeling of contentment because I am grateful that she and I both have mouths to speak with and healthy minds with which to reason.

To experience lasting happiness is to experience inner peace and emotional stability by actively thinking, feeling, and behaving in ways that are loving and kind to ourselves and others. Happiness is not something external to be searched for and sought after. It is an internal journey, a way of being, and a lifestyle. It is actively being at peace with yourself and your circumstances, whatever they may be. It is about making appropriate changes when and where it is possible.

Please don't confuse being at peace with circumstances as settling for less. To settle is to be inactive and no longer accept responsibility for your life. To be at peace with your circumstance is to know that you can gracefully weather whatever storm that life presents. You do not have to wait on a change in circumstances to be content and at peace. For me, it means that I have already done the best that I could in any given situation, and there is nothing else that I could physically do to effect meaningful change. It is a habit for me to give my best, which might not be perfect at the time, but it is what I'm willing and able to offer given my current obligations and circumstances.

'If you are going to pray, don't worry,
and if you are going to worry, then don't pray.'
— Anonymous proverb

AFTER ACCEPTING THAT I'VE DONE all that I can physically do, my next move is to breathe in and relax my body, breathe out, and smile: Now is the time to surrender to the God of my understanding. Feel free to change 'God of my understanding' to whatever source or higher power works for you. I can now relax because I am no longer trying to figure out something that is out of my control. An old wise saying is, 'If you are going to pray, don't worry, and if you are going to worry, then don't pray.' I've had to remind myself of this statement and use it as a mantra many times in my life, especially when it came to dealing with other people's behavior or health concerns.

Every individual has the capacity to create her inner world of joy by taking ownership of her happiness and increasing awareness of her thoughts, feelings, and behaviors. If you truly want to experience a lifestyle of happiness, then commit to experiencing happiness despite external circumstances. It is a simple question to ask yourself, 'Do I want to experience inner peace and happiness?' If the answer is yes, then you are willing to let go of things that don't matter and able to manage the things that do matter.

Major changes will occur in life. Your partner may cheat on you. Your child may go to jail. You might be diagnosed with a health concern. None of these changes have to steal your happiness. It is still up to you to fulfill your commitment to yourself to experience happiness.

Practice making daily commitments to internal happiness. Take it one day at a time. Your happiness is contingent upon you and your actions, not your external situation and things that happen outside you. How do you think people survived and made extraordinary recoveries from traumatic events such as the Holocaust, slavery, rape, and natural disasters?

The Search

OUR MINDS REVEL in playing games with us. We don't feel settled, centered, and grounded. Our minds continually think about the greener grass on the other side of the fence. What if we moved to another state? What if we changed jobs? What if we changed partners? We would then be happy, right? Many people have made significant life changes and still did not feel settled. You are grounded and centered wherever you are because wherever you go, there you are. You can't run from your Self.

'Do not confuse motion and progress. A rocking horse keeps moving but does not make any progress.'
— Alfred A. Montapert

WOULD YOU BE HAPPY WITH a highly stressful job that paid a lot of money? Would you be happy with a less stressful job that paid less money? If neither of these situations would bring you happiness, then I challenge you to evaluate what would bring you happiness. No situation will be perfect. No relationship will be perfect. No job will be perfect. When will you stop searching and allow yourself to be at peace with the concept of just being present, grateful, and aware?

Eckhart Tolle uses the word *isness* to describe what is going on right now, at this very moment. It is healthy for us to participate fully in the power of Now, allowing *isness* to simply be as it is. We are human beings, not human doings. Be mindful of getting lost in doing a lot of things that do not matter, such as scrolling through social media and engaging in gossip. Slow down on doing so much and practice being right here, right now, where you have everything that you need in this moment.

Have you ever wondered why you thought you would be happy once something happened, such as a new job, and once you obtained your wish, you still felt unhappy? This feeling is called *hedonic adaptation*, which is when you no longer experience positive emotions from an event that once made you extremely happy.

LYUBOMIRSKY'S RESEARCH HAS SHOWN that lasting happiness is not found in changing our circumstances. A positive change in our circumstances will increase our positive mood and pleasurable feelings only temporarily. By the same principle—and this will be good news for many of us—a negative change in circumstances typically has a minimal impact on our overall happiness. We will eventually return to the same emotional state that we maintained before experiencing the change in circumstances.

Mindful Acceptance as a form of emotional self-care could help increase your state of happiness. You will no longer search for happiness somewhere outside yourself, but by vigorously pursuing your values and meeting value-driven goals you will experience lasting happiness and success.

Best Self in Action: Happiness myths

IF WE ARE TO ENGAGE IN EMOTIONAL SELF-CARE, we will need to be mindful of some common happiness myths. Notice if you believe any of the following statements. In order to experience happiness, I must:

- Achieve certain milestones before I can experience happiness.
- Only experience positive circumstances, and not experience any adversities, setbacks, or failures.
- Always experience joy and positive feelings and never experience sadness, fear, or anxiety.
- Control my emotions such as fear and anxiety and my thoughts, especially the negative ones.

TAKE A MOMENT TO REALLY CONSIDER the last time you thought, 'I'll be happy when.' Think about the last time you told yourself that you would be happy when you achieved some goal. Did this achievement make you happy? If so, how long were you happy? Do you think this event helped you achieve lasting happiness, or did it just temporarily boost your positive emotions?

Try to complete the 'I will be happy when' exercise for different life events. It will help you contrast what truly increases your deep-seated happiness with what makes you feel good or happy for brief periods of time.

To experience lasting happiness, practice a daily commitment to internal stability and peace. This means that you commit to peace unconditionally. No matter what happens to you throughout the day, you are centered and grounded enough to be unmoved. Successful people recommit if commitments are broken. This skill works best when practiced one day at a time.

6

THE FOUR DISCIPLINES

THE FOUR DISCIPLINES OF MINDFUL ACCEPTANCE are beautifully interdependent. *Mindfulness* empowers the ability to be creative, intentional, and self-compassionate. *Creativity* seeks new ways to be mindful, intentional, and self-compassionate. *Intention* gives direction to mindfulness, self-compassion, and creativity. *Self-compassion* gives us the patience we need to practice mindfulness, intention, and creativity with courage and gentleness. Mindful Acceptance is an engaged and active form of mindfulness.

'You can't heal what you never reveal.'
— Jay-Z

AWARENESS IS A PREREQUISITE for changing, coping, and ending our resistance to reality. If you are unaware of a problem or concern, then how can you deal with it? Awareness alone is not enough to cope with the imperfections of ourselves, relationships, others, and the world, but it is a great start!

Mindfulness: Affirming the present moment

THERE ARE MANY DEFINITIONS FOR *MINDFULNESS*. Some definitions seem to suggest that mindfulness appears to be the awareness of whatever your mind wants to think, while other definitions explain mindfulness as more intentional and focused. Jon Kabat-Zinn, founder of the Mindfulness-Based Stress Reduction program, defines mindfulness as 'awareness that arises through paying attention, on purpose, in the present moment, non-judgmentally.' Further, he says that mindfulness is 'about knowing what is on your mind.' Russ Harris sums up mindfulness as 'consciously bringing awareness to your here and now experience, with openness, receptiveness, and interest.'

Mindfulness means focusing on your personal reality, including your strengths and limitations, the reality of relationships, and the reality of the world. Mindfulness informs our ability to see and acknowledge 'what is.' The acknowledgement of reality doesn't have to be a big production, but it is a wholehearted realization that you have about your Self without any self-denial. Sometimes, in the short-term, it appears safer to live in denial, where conflict is avoided and there is the illusion of peace. However, long-term costs often outweigh short-term relief.

Many people are turned off by the thought of mindfulness because they may associate it with formal Eastern religious meditation practices found in Buddhism or Taoism. Informal mindfulness lacks a religious or philosophical element, making it acceptable to people of all faiths, occupations, and cultures. Western psychology, especially *acceptance and commitment therapy*, relies heavily on informal mindfulness to achieve some of the same benefits as formal mindfulness without the religious undertones and intensive time commitment.

Informal mindfulness is a process where we intentionally notice and observe our stream of thoughts and focus on what is going on in the present. I love to practice informal mindfulness on my walks in my neighborhood. It is easy for me to get lost in replaying events of the day or planning for the future. When this happens, I intentionally remind myself to enjoy my present moment. I do not attempt to get rid of thoughts concerning what already happened and what needs to happen. I just notice that my mind is active and say to myself, 'My mind is active,' which creates space for me to notice how I am feeling right now.

Once I tap into the present moment, I realize that everything is perfect and serene. At this moment, there are no worries about the past or future. There is just the wonderful now. On my walks, I delight in the beauty of the sky, trees, leaves, flowers, and grass. There is the humor of watching the squirrels run around and play. I feel the gentle breeze and warm sun on my skin. All of this is amazing if I am willing to notice it. This small task of noticing my environment is a form of emotional self-care because I have given my mind a break from fighting, resisting, and working. My mind is simply allowed 'to be' in the present within the discipline of Mindful Acceptance.

Being mindful can be strengthened by increasing and practicing mindfulness skills that focus on the present moment-to-moment experiences of what is going on right now. Donald Altman, in *The Mindfulness Toolbox*, breaks down different mindfulness activities that may work for different learning styles. He suggests that not every mindfulness practice will have the same results for each person. A language-oriented person might benefit from mindfulness practices that include thoughts, words, and storytelling. Someone who is spatially oriented might benefit more from a movement mindfulness practice such as mindful walking or yoga.

Thich Nhat Hanh does a beautiful job encouraging us to be mindful in our everyday lives in his practical guide, *Peace is Every Step*. Hanh asks us to increase our awareness of our breath, which is always with us. It seems so simple, but so often we overlook conscious breathing.

The skill that I like most is the combined breathing and smiling practice. Hanh encourages us to breathe in calm and breathe out a smile. I have found myself practicing this skill throughout my day during non-stressful and stressful moments. Smiling changes my facial structure, posture, and mood. Breathing and smiling helps me position myself in an emotional space where I can make vital decisions that take me in the direction of what matters most to me—my values. Recently, while I was driving, my younger daughter was giving me a hard time. I said out loud, 'Breathe in, I relax my body; breathe out, I smile.' My older daughter informed me that her sister was plugging her ears. I told her that my breathing exercise was not for her sister, but for me.

Increasing mindfulness skills and being mindful of past and present reality will put you on the path to making constructive decisions that have a direct impact on your emotions, self-acceptance, relationships, and overall happiness.

MANY OF US LIVE SUCH FAST-PACED LIVES that we don't have time to stop and smell the flowers, cook a healthy meal, read a book, or even play with our children. The practice of Mindful Acceptance encourages us to be intentional about stepping away from our busy lives and just be present with ourselves, loved ones, and the world. A great way to reconnect with the people in your household is to practice unplugging when you are together. I try not to be on my phone until after my children are in bed. How can I encourage them to limit their media time if I am unable to limit mine?

Mindfulness skills will help you create mental space for greatness, creativity, flexibility, and emotional self-care. Everyday mindfulness invites you to give your full attention to whatever you are doing. Everyday mindfulness activities include stretching and focusing on your breathing before getting out of bed, slowly and intentionally making up your bed in the morning, brushing your teeth with your less dominant hand, driving your vehicle, cleaning your home, writing, drawing, singing and dancing, and yes, coloring in adult coloring books. While doing these activities, your mind will wander to planning, evaluating, or problem-solving. When it wanders, just gently bring your attention back to the task at hand. Practice just noticing your mind as it wanders to a past or future event and kindly bringing it back to what you are doing. These mindfulness activities will help strengthen your ability to focus attention where you want to focus it, such as on completing a project.

These activities will help you understand that you do not have to interpret every thought that travels through your mind. You will learn to keep destructive and irrational thoughts at a distance. Increasing mindfulness skills and being mindful of past and present reality will put you on the path to making constructive decisions that have a direct impact on your emotions, self-acceptance, relationships, and overall happiness.

'Yesterday is history. Tomorrow is a mystery.
Today is a gift. That's why it's called The Present.'
— Anonymous proverb

BEING MINDFUL IN OUR DAY-TO-DAY activities will increase emotional self-care and allow us to enjoy the present. Have you ever been in the heat of the moment and said or done mean things that when you later thought about it, you wish you had been more thoughtful and mindful, such as yelling at your child, being physically aggressive, or engaging in risky behavior? Present moments of life are precious gifts that we need to cherish, giving our minds a break from thinking about the past or worrying about the future. There is great wisdom in the anonymous proverb, 'Yesterday is history. Tomorrow is a mystery. Today is a gift, that's why it is called The Present.'

Being mindful allows you to be flexible and creative about where you focus your attention. Mindful Acceptance is an active focus, while at the same time being compassionate towards your mind when it becomes unfocused. Just as you are mindful of your physical limitations and know that you have to work diligently to build up your muscle strength, I encourage you to become patient with the limits of your mind and begin practicing mindfulness skills to build your mental muscle.

The practice of mindfulness will help us get in touch with our bodies. When we are running full speed ahead, often on fumes, it becomes difficult to hear what our bodies are telling us. If you have worked a full work week, volunteered with your organizations, and helped family, your body might be exhausted on the weekend. If you are dragging on Saturday morning and there is nothing pressing that needs to be done, it will do your body some good to get some extra rest.

If you have a judgmental mind that tells you that only lazy people sleep in, mindfulness skills will help you notice the unhelpful thought and allow you to give yourself what you need in that moment. You could choose to sleep an extra hour rather than half the day. In this situation, if you cannot shake the thought that you *should* be doing something other than sleeping, try being creative about getting the rest you need. You could try tricking your mind into accepting that you will only be resting for a short period of time by setting a timer for the amount of time that you sleep late.

A word of caution. Our bodies will tell us when we are doing too much, and it is our responsibility to listen. My body lets me know that I need to slow down when I experience flu-like symptoms for 24 hours. That is just enough time to *make* me slow down and rest. Be mindful that your body will get the rest it needs by force or choice.

I know some people who take B12 shots to keep them going when they are fatigued. If you have been busy and your body alerts you that you need to rest, consider trusting your body and being kind to it. Energy drinks, shots, and pills do not encourage emotional self-care, but instead create a habit of overexertion and burnout.

AIMEE'S MOTHER RECENTLY PASSED from a tragic accident. Everything happened so suddenly that she didn't have time to process the tragedy. Two months after her mother's passing, Aimee was sitting at her desk at work and became over-whelmed with emotions. She sat there fighting back tears until she decided to listen to her body, excuse herself, and go to the bathroom to cry. She felt much better and was more productive at work after allowing her body to feel grief and do what it needed to do.

'Mindfulness isn't difficult,
we just need to remember to do it.'
— *Sharon Salzberg*

WHEN WE ARE BUSY AND HUNGRY, it becomes difficult to make healthy food choices. Our busy lives don't allow us time to wash and cut up fresh fruit at night to take with us the next day. Our busy lives don't lend itself to morning smoothies or hot breakfasts. We blast through our days without noticing hunger pains. When we are finally able to slow down, we are too hungry to make a healthy food decision. When we are starving, we grab the first fast food in sight. Had we slowed down earlier and listened to our bodies, we would have had the opportunity to notice what our bellies were telling us and make healthier food choices.

Our bodies know what it needs; we just need to listen to it. When we are able to slow down, breathe, and listen, we will be able to support the needs of our bodies. Mindfulness will help us listen to our bodies as a form of emotional self-care.

We can benefit from choosing to be mindful of our past reality without slipping into unhealthy self-criticism. We can choose to be mindful of our current circumstances without being melancholy. We can choose to be mindful of what the future might hold without being overwhelmed. The process of being mindful will keep us aware of our experiences and of our thoughts in the present moment.

Intentionality: Engaging the situation

MINDFUL ACCEPTANCE INVITES US to take an active role in our mental environment by taking charge of our situation and committing to intentional action. Mindfulness creates the space needed for increasing skillful thoughts and behaviors and holding unpleasant thoughts and emotions gently. Mindfulness activities increase focus on what is currently going on inside, outside, and around our bodies. Intentionality takes it a step further and chooses what to attend to and what behavior to engage. Being mindful puts you on the path to success, while intentionality moves you along that path.

Intentionality is the committed action of Mindful Acceptance. Intentionality is purposeful action. We can commit to increasing positive and realistic thoughts and engaging in meaningful behaviors in the service of living a productive, satisfying, and vital life. Being intentional means making a personal commitment to taking action on behalf of our well-being. Action could be an observable act, or it could be a private experience, such as self-talk. Doing something could mean being patient. As long as it is intentional, it is doing something. Jon Kabat-Zinn, in *Wherever You Go, There You Are,* describes patience as an attitude that can be cultivated. To enhance my patience, I practice relaxing my mind, body, and emotions by engaging in conscious breathing, smiling, and focusing on the big picture of situations.

How do I increase my self-worth
and feel better about myself?

MANY PEOPLE HAVE STRUGGLED WITH finding a solution to this conundrum because they are overly focused on trying to change how they *think* and *feel*. I encourage people to be intentional about changing how they behave, and over time, it will have an effect on how they automatically feel, think, and behave. Intentional behavior can create automatic thoughts.

Consider making small daily commitments to engage in emotional self-care. Commitments turn into habits. Be mindful that research suggests that it takes at least 21 days to make something a habit. Once behaviors have become habits, you no longer have to think about them. Emotional self-care includes making a commitment to repeat daily mantras:

- I can be scared and do what's important to me.
- I'm going to run my race.
- This is just a feeling; it can't hurt me.

YOU COULD COMMIT TO making small goals for yourself and achieving them. These commitments will provide you with real-life evidence that you are capable and competent, which increases how you feel about yourself. Behaviors have more impact on emotions than emotions have on behavior.

Intentionality allows us to let go of trying to change what is outside our power to change, and move forward with decision-making, and take action. Intentionality will help us commit to healthy behaviors. Most importantly, it will help us recommit when we have fallen off the proverbial wagon. Recommitting is just as important as the initial commitment.

Self-Compassion: Loving your Self

COMPASSION IS OFTEN THOUGHT OF as having sympathy for oneself and others. The discipline of self-compassion in Mindful Acceptance goes way beyond having sympathy for your suffering and pain. Self-compassion means holding hands with our pain without the experience becoming overwhelming.

Self-compassion is a skill that can be learned and cultivated. Learning self-compassion helps us engage in healthy boundaries when dealing with other people because we are able to feel their pain without getting lost in it. Self-compassion empowers us to make decisions that are respectful to ourselves and others.

Kristin Neff, in her lovely book, *Self-Compassion*, looks beyond the normal definitions of self-compassion and extends it to be attainable to all people. She defines self-compassion as having three core parts: self-kindness, recognition of our common humanity, and mindfulness. Self-compassion encourages us to direct kind and gentle thoughts and behaviors towards ourselves. It discourages us from being judgmental and negative. As we are being mindful of our thoughts, we will encounter beliefs that are painful and unhealthy, revealing negative behaviors or thoughts. Self-compassion enables us to encounter these thoughts with patience and tenderness. Mindful Acceptance teaches us to face a reality that is sometimes unkind. Self-compassion is the antithesis of self-criticisms and self-judgments, offering grace and mercy to ourselves when we make a mistake and gently providing us with the strength necessary to make better decisions.

Self-compassion empowers us to be intentional.

AISHA ONCE SHARED WITH ME a pattern of behavior that she had noticed about herself. She often thought that she was not as intelligent as other people. She would be so anxious and concerned about sounding stupid in conversing with new people that she would stumble over her words and lose her train of thought. She said that these types of examples would confirm that she was stupid. In this situation, if Aisha would embrace unrelenting self-compassion, she could prevent this social anxiety from continuing to be an issue for her.

We often unintentionally embody what we say to ourselves, so we need to be mindful of the thoughts that we nourish. If our inner dialogue is not taken too seriously, we can allow ourselves to be fully human: wonderfully made, talented, and inherently flawed. By affirming our humanity, we can all allow for mistakes and celebrate our potential for greatness. The practice of self-compassion will prevent us from getting stuck in destructive or false things that we say about ourselves. We will continue to move forward, and self-compassion allows us to do this with minor bumps in the road. Do you have any intentional and compassionate statements that you use when you make *human* mistakes to help you cope with the consequences?

My favorite intentional and compassionate statement is: *Going forward, I will do better.* I am intentional about choosing not to over identify with thoughts that are punitive and shaming.

By affirming our humanity, we can all allow for mistakes and celebrate our potential for greatness.

AS A CLINICIAN, compassion has to be a priority in helping my clients adopt Mindful Acceptance to their situations. If you have been diagnosed with a chronic condition, I can't tell you to make friends with your condition. That would be the opposite of compassion, and rather insensitive. First, I must validate and convey that I understand your story and situation. Then, it will be important for me to convey my compassion for your situation by expressing that I could imagine how painful you might feel. I would only mention embracing the chronic condition after the outpour of genuine compassion. Acceptance cannot live and flourish without compassion.

Self-compassion frees up mental space for us to be creative. A loud and busy mind that is filled with judgments and criticisms will have a difficult time creatively exploring options for effective decision-making. We begin practicing self-compassion by actively looking for the pain and suffering behind our thoughts and behavior. Many of us are able to recognize pain as a universal human experience and empathize with it. Looking at our own pain helps us to take a step back or distance ourselves from our situation so that we can address the pain. When offering compassion to others, recognizing their pain helps us to realize that we are more similar than dissimilar. As a result, we are less likely to judge other people.

Creativity: Choosing the best path

THE PSYCHOLOGICAL CONCEPT OF CREATIVITY doesn't have anything to do with being artsy. It has everything to do with being flexible, curious, and open to all behaviors that are within your value system. Creativity allows us to think beyond our limits. A creative mindset explores and exhausts all valuable options. Mindfulness helps us to increase awareness of what we can and cannot change while creativity helps us think beyond what we can see, touch, and feel within our realm of behavior change.

If we have a creative mindset, we will be able to see beyond any tough situation. As the saying goes, 'Life happens,' and it happens to all of us. Life will continue to happen, and we need to be prepared to explore all our options when it does.

It is common for young people to leave the community of their nucleus family and begin their own family in a different state. There is some truth to the adage, 'It takes a village to raise a family,' and many young people are missing the support of their communities. The young people who have moved away from their families are often lonely and sad about not having any family nearby. Being creative in this situation includes creating a support system by developing intimate friendships and initiating mentorships. I encourage you to be creative about making friends and nurturing the relationships so much that your friends become the family of your choosing.

Being creative means that we will never settle for less than what we deserve because we do not see any other options. When we have a creative mindset, we will always be able to choose a path that is full of possibilities, meaning, and fulfillment.

Creativity is especially useful in handling the negative effects of job stress. Research indicates that job stress can contribute to chronic health problems, such as psychological disorders, musculoskeletal disorders, and cardiovascular disease. Many people think that they are overworked and underpaid. They are working in environments where they have little to no control. The doom and gloom of the current job market make the workplace the perfect case study for creativity.

Being creative means
that we will never settle for less than what we deserve
because we do not see any other options.

ANITA WORKED IN CORPORATE AMERICA as an underwriter where the bank wanted her to review loans, answer phones, and meet an unreasonable quota. Anita was struggling to keep up and barely had time to relieve herself without her supervisor looking for her. At the end of the long day, she was drained and didn't have anything left to give to herself or her friends. She wanted to be in a romantic relationship, but she didn't feel like going out to meet people.

Anita gave up on taking care of her physical self and having a life outside work. She was overweight and had high blood pressure. She was at risk for losing her job because she was engaging in frequent crying spells and not meeting her quota.

Anita explored ways to creatively meet some of her needs on and off the job. Anita determined that being active was important to her. Given that her office job was sedentary, she began to take mental and physical breaks by standing up and engaging in conscious breathing every couple of hours. Anita used the *Breathe* app on her Apple watch to coach her through a breathing exercise. She began to feel better equipped to deal with some of the work stress just by giving her mind and body a break every couple of hours. Her work experience proved to her that she could find peace in any situation, even a toxic work environment. Anita's sense of peace during her emotional storm provided her the strength to look for another job, which she did successfully. Anita decided to make time for a social life. She created an online profile, began dating, and eventually married and had children.

HAVE YOU EVER NOTICED the quality of the decisions that you have made when you thought you had no other options? These decisions probably weren't in your best interest. Being creative acknowledges sticky situations, but always explores options that are outside the box.

Being creative means that we are willing to try, and willing to fail. A major difference between successful people and people who are not is that successful people are persistent. In order to be persistent, you have to be creative. Creativity will allow you to try different behaviors until the best behavior produces the desired outcome.

Most people are not lucky enough to boast about success that occurred with one try. We have to try, try, and try again before we enjoy success. The path to success is challenging! It is what it is! We have to Mindfully Accept that life is challenging and affirm that we can be intentional and creative about overcoming each and every obstacle, every time! Being creative transforms hurdles into opportunities to grow.

A past client, Herman, came to see me about his partner's argumentativeness. Herman said, 'She wants to dispute everything. I wish she would understand that not everything needs a long-winded retort or remark.' They would start talking about a small thing that he didn't do to his partner's satisfaction, such as not paying a bill when she said to pay it. Then, the small situation would turn into something explosive. Herman and I explored ways that he could creatively choose how to deal with her. First, Herman needed a skill to help prevent him from getting sucked into verbal sparring. He learned to pause and notice what was going on inside his body and take gentle breaths before he responded to his partner.

Herman chose to be intentional about communicating limits as to when and where they would have these types of intense discussions. He became intentional about not having heated discussions in front of their children. Herman committed to participating in fewer arguments. After all, it takes two to argue. Ultimately, Herman chose creative ways to end, avert, or delay the conversations. During times when Herman's guard was down, and he lost his composure in verbal altercations, he began to practice self-compassion and calming self-talk.

Over time, Herman experienced less tension and stress in his relationship, mainly due to him changing his behavior and taking a compassionate stance. No longer did Herman blame his partner for his emotions. He began to take charge of his situation, emotions, and life.

Best Self in Action: Being mindful in real life

YOUR LIFE CAN BE ENHANCED by practicing the four disciplines of Mindful Acceptance. The first step in any behavior change is to increase awareness. Acknowledge what is outside your control, expand your capacity to allow 'what is,' and still do the things that matter.

We can only change *our* behavior. We have to allow other people to be who they are, and intentionally engage in behavior that leads us on the path to success.

Commit to letting go of relationships and beliefs that are not working for you and cultivating relationships and beliefs that are likely to work for you.

Life isn't fair. Don't allow your awareness of the unfairness of life to get in the way of your success and happiness.

All of us are visited by disturbing thoughts from time to time. If we allow these thoughts to overwhelm us and create knots, then we might engage in behaviors that are not in the direction of what is most important to us.

THE GIFTS OF EMOTIONAL SELF-CARE

EMOTIONAL SELF-CARE HELPS US MAKE DECISIONS that will bring us satisfaction, fulfillment, and vitality. You have the power to cultivate these gifts, and watch them transform you and the world around you. Today is the day to tap into your gifts and live the life of your choosing. The future is not promised to any of us. The only guarantee that we have is right now. The *now* consists of what you see, feel, taste, touch, and experience in this very moment.

---

*'The curious paradox is that when
I accept myself just as I am, then I can change.'*
— *Carl Rogers*

MANY PEOPLE ARE WAITING on someone else to accept, respect, love, and show compassion to them before they begin fully loving and enjoying life. The secret is that these gifts are already within us. We can fully accept, respect, and love ourselves by practicing emotional self-care. Once we fully accept ourselves and our situations, we can work on changing what we can change.

Accepting your whole Self

IF YOU FIND IT DIFFICULT to accept certain aspects of your Self, such as your predispositions, automatic thoughts, and natural emotions, begin to notice what your mind is telling you that is getting in the way of self-acceptance. Then, ask yourself, 'Is it helpful for me to take seriously what my mind is telling me in this very moment?' If the answer is yes, then go with it and allow the thought to help you to do your best. If the answer is no, then you may want to consider the practice of allowing unhealthy thoughts to come and go like waves in the ocean.

We function as our Best Self when we bring our whole Self to the situation. Practice behaving from a place of flexibility while avoiding rigidity and extremes. This middle way behavior will allow us to integrate all aspects of ourselves in moderation. We appear out of sorts when we are living in extremes. Extreme behaviors get in the way of integration because of the pain of swinging from one extreme to another. Extreme behaviors cannot persist for extended periods of time, so practice moderation as a skill of self-acceptance and integration.

The mere acknowledgment of a thought being a thought will help you realize that you do not have to obey your thoughts.

MINDFUL ACCEPTANCE INVITES YOU to apply the *acceptance and commitment therapy* skill of looking *at* your thoughts and not *from* your thoughts. Don't resist your thoughts. Just notice them. Take some deep breaths. Breathe in calm and peace. Breathe out unhealthy thoughts to loosen their hold on you and smile. It's hard to smile and be tense at the same time. Smiling will help loosen and relax your body. This practice of conscious breathing and smiling when your mind is not being friendly will help prevent you from forming internal hot buttons.

Respecting your inner being

IF WE FEEL LIKE PEOPLE are disrespecting us, let's make sure we are demonstrating respect for ourselves. We can't control other people's behavior, but we can certainly control our own behavior by asserting ourselves in situations where we feel people are being disrespectful. If someone is speaking to us in a condescending and belittling tone, we can immediately inform the other person that we will not tolerate that behavior. If the person doesn't stop speaking to us in a demeaning tone after we have addressed the situation, we can end the conversation until the other person agrees to speak in a respectful tone. It is our responsibility to inform other people how to treat us. Let's not leave how we are treated by others up to chance.

We can show respect for ourselves by prioritizing our emotional needs. If Brandon is reserved and likes to spend time alone, it would be disrespectful to himself if he allowed someone to bully him into spending time with large groups of people. Brandon would benefit from expressing his need for solitude and saying 'no' in situations that went against his needs at the given moment.

'No' is a complete sentence.
It does not require justification or explanation.

ONE WAY TO DEMONSTRATE SELF-RESPECT includes valuing the boundaries of our time. First, identify and prioritize your social roles. Then, notice how much time is being given to each role. Next, decide whether you value your time as a form of emotional self-care. If so, make sure that you are reserving some time for engaging in your own mental health and emotional well-being. Don't forget to be mindful of how you are using your time; don't waste it on frivolous activities. It might be helpful to limit the time spent on social media, television, and other mindless activities. For some people, unplugging during certain times of the day is emotional self-care. Pour some of your time back into your Self, and you will be in a genuine place to spend time with others.

You need to know your physical and emotional limits so that you are able to protect and respect them. Remember that you can only be in one place at a time. Many people overcommit in good faith, but let others down because of an inability to fulfill all the accepted requests. Many people who overcommit often find it difficult to be punctual because they have so much to do in a seemingly small amount of time. The solution is to only take on what you know you can handle given your current obligations and responsibilities.

Loving your Self

IF YOU FEEL LONELY AND UNLOVABLE, you can show love for your Self by engaging in loving thoughts and behaviors such as encouraging, supportive, and kind self-talk. If a situation is challenging, it might be helpful to give attention to thoughts that can motivate you to move toward your goal: 'I have successfully conquered difficult situations in the past, and I can do it again.' Several of my clients who identify as Christians quote Philippians 4:13, 'I can do all things through Christ who strengthens me.'

Loving behaviors, such as setting boundaries, can prevent violations that leave you feeling used and abused. Without proper boundaries, we convey to others that we are unworthy and underserving of love and respect. Even if we don't completely believe that we are worthy and lovable, let's act like we are worthy until our mind begins to agree. Loving behaviors include dropping the internal struggle within yourself and strengthening your mental capacity to allow guilt-ridden emotions and thoughts to come and go so that you can engage in emotional self-care.

Being grateful for who you are

INTENTIONALLY INCORPORATING GRATITUDE in our daily lives is one of the easiest ways to cultivate our inner power. I recently said to myself 'I'm so tired of people talking about gratitude, including myself. It's like the new buzz word.' The irony is that I can't stop touting the importance of practicing gratitude as a habit of happiness. Gratitude is an attitude of thankfulness and an intentional focus on the positive, if focusing on the positive doesn't cause personal harm (for example, being positive about an abusive relationship). Gratitude doesn't cost any money or require a lot of time. It is easily accessible and can be cultivated anytime and anywhere.

An easy gratitude skill is to increase awareness of breath. The gratitude of breath is a good place to begin each morning. Every day that we are granted the privilege of waking up to a new day, we have something to be grateful for. Before you get out of bed, practice noticing your breath. Notice if it is hot, warm, or stale. Allow yourself to smile. You have something to be grateful for. Without breath, the possibility for happiness, meaning, and satisfaction ends in this lifetime. Breath opens the door to the possibilities of the internal and external world.

The concept of gratitude has been extensively researched. Robert Emmons, an expert on gratitude, and his colleagues have helped people cultivate gratitude, usually by keeping a gratitude journal. Emmons and his colleagues found that the practice of gratitude increases one's ability to get enough exercise and adequate sleep, experience positive emotions and happiness, and develop stronger relationships with others.

I FREQUENTLY ASK MY CLIENTS if they are willing to begin the practice of gratitude by keeping a journal as a homework assignment. If they agree and find it helpful, I will ask them to continue maintaining a gratitude journal until the attitude of gratitude becomes automatic. Several of my clients have benefitted from gratitude journals, but I will share Paige's story. She reluctantly came to see me because she thought her issue was minor in comparison to others. She explained that nothing was really wrong with her *per se*; she just did not experience happiness.

Paige was under the impression that other people woke up every day feeling happy as a default mental state. Paige tended to focus on the negative aspects of her life. Instead of trying to didactically explore all the positive aspects of Paige's life with her, I asked her if she were willing to keep a gratitude journal by writing down three positive things about her day before going to bed and reading it the next morning.

In addition to the gratitude journal, I discussed the *gratitude of breath* concept with Paige. Within a week, she was so impressed with her change in mood that she continued with the activities for the next month. The purpose of these activities was to help Paige look at her life from a different perspective so that she would be better equipped to live a more fulfilling life. She did become intentional about taking a mental gratitude inventory and incorporating *gratitude of breath* when she felt herself sliding into an emotional slump, refusing to engage in behaviors that were meaningful, or feeling bored with life.

Gratitude could become the go-to coping tool to deal with life. It is very easy to get caught up in the woes and throes of life. Life is absolutely not perfect. We have to be armed with emotional self-care tools to cope with the storms of life.

Laughing at your Self and with your Self

LAUGHTER IS GOOD FOR THE SOUL. Laughter boosts our immune system, calms our body, slows down our flight or fight responses, triggers the release of endorphins, increases heart health, and reduces anger. Given the many benefits of laughter, we may want to consider adding some humor and laughter into our daily lives.

Humor is the ability to see, express, or experience something that is funny. I've heard some people say that they don't laugh often because they don't have a sense of humor. I do not encourage us to sit around exploring and analyzing why we don't seem to have a sense of humor. I suggest that we begin laughing now and discover that our sense of humor increases as a by-product of laughter. Humor is often the cause of laughter, but it doesn't have to be present before we begin laughing.

Self-laughter is a great form of emotional self-care.

When we are able to laugh at ourselves, we are not taking our *selves* too seriously. We take ourselves so seriously that we won't allow ourselves to laugh at mishaps. The next time that you are in an embarrassing situation, try laughing instead of beating yourself up and searching for an exit. People will often laugh with you, not at you, in an embarrassing situation. They may share a similar situation that happened to them.

If you don't like people laughing at you because you think that something must be wrong with you, try not to hold this thought too tightly. Instead, catch the laughter and enjoy its benefits. Self-laughter is a great form of emotional self-care. You don't always have to laugh out loud; you can laugh or smile to yourself.

Practice turning your mouth upward into a smile, and then laughing at yourself for randomly doing it. If you would like to cultivate a sense of humor, just notice the present moment. Go with the flow.

We often wonder why some people are more resilient than others. Laughter is one of the mediating factors. Laughter helps position us in the mental space to reassess our current situation, engage in perspective taking, and let go of unnecessary mental weight.

We don't need to have a great sense of humor in order to laugh. If we want to cultivate humor, life will present us with opportunities to notice it in many situations. My daughter once noticed that she did not have her backpack when we were halfway to her school. I turned around to go back home for it. As I was getting out the truck to get her backpack, she asked me to grab a water bottle for her. Apparently, I was distracted. I returned from the house and gave my daughter her water bottle. About halfway to school again, I asked her to put something in her backpack. Can you believe that I left it again? I didn't have a choice but to laugh at myself.

Supporting each other

EMOTIONAL SELF-CARE affirms the importance of having supportive people in our lives. As we are healing ourselves, we are becoming better for others. We are increasing our awareness of ourselves and no longer arguing about unspoken issues. We are creating healthy boundaries so that we can respect and love ourselves as well as others.

A healthy social support system can make the difference between life and death. Research with cancer patients who received emotional support and those who did not revealed that patients who felt supported adjusted better. The National Cancer Institute states, 'some research shows that joining a support group improves both quality of life and survival.' The advent of support groups all over the world highlights the importance of a social support system.

Emotional self-care acknowledges
the importance of a social support system.

I ENCOURAGE YOU to have a select group of friends who have proven trustworthy when it comes to you being vulnerable, real, and genuinely human. It is helpful to turn to them for emotional support when you need non-judgmental and compassionate listeners. Find people who compassionately tell it like it is, and aren't easily moved when you vent in an unfiltered and uncensored manner. I encourage everyone to be intentional about creating the space for this type of company. Be mindful that in order to create space, we often have to let go of whatever it is taking up unnecessary mental and physical occupancy. It could be letting go of toxic people or stories about yourself that are not helpful. Making space entails a willingness to let go of what is not working in your life and creating an openness to receive what and who the Universe has to offer.

Best Self in Action: Engaging your gifts

SOMETIMES PEOPLE DON'T REALIZE IT, but taking care of your mind, body, and soul could be a valued action for you to choose for yourself. The mental, emotional, and spiritual aspects are the subtle and often neglected parts of the Self. The same way that we would nurture our physical body needs to be the same way we would show concern for our emotional Self. If you have chosen valuing yourself as a life value and want to commit to an action of self-care, then writing down your goal is a meaningful way to meet your need.

Which emotional self-care practices can you commit to implementing into your life from each category in the list below?

Physical examples include exercising regularly, eating nutritious meals, getting adequate sleep, resting, and taking medications appropriately.

Mental examples include watching your thinking, cultivating positive and realistic thoughts, seeking the humor in your thoughts, journaling, and looking *at your thoughts, not from your thoughts.*

Emotional examples include allowing the movement of uncomfortable thoughts and emotions to come and go, asserting yourself, increasing boundaries, learning to say no when you are unable to help, increasing gratitude, forgiving yourself, and engaging in mindfulness activities such as mindful walking, mindful eating, and mindful listening.

Spiritual examples include cultivating healthy relationships with others, praying, meditating, or adopting a relationship with a power greater than yourself, observing the beauty of non-human sentient and living things, noticing the world in which you live with awe and curiosity, and listening to inspirational music.

8

The Reclaimed *Self*

H UMAN BEINGS ARE NOT PERFECT CREATURES. Unconditional self-acceptance is the functional embrace of all
our imperfections. Some days will be harder than others to
engage in emotional self-care. When you begin to practice the
disciplines of Mindful Acceptance, the difficult days will be
more manageable.

JEREMY STRUGGLED with intrusive thoughts that were aggressive and violent. He was afraid to reveal his thoughts to family
and close friends because he felt that they would be scared and
uncomfortable. Jeremy consulted me because he felt that he
was beginning to lose his mind. I assisted Jeremy by providing

him with a safe place to explore his mental environment. We worked on being intentional about creating calming and de-escalating thoughts. We did not focus on attempting to get rid of intrusive thoughts, but to distance himself from them to re-group and make the best decisions. Most importantly, we spent a lot of time working on self-acceptance and self-compassion. These concepts were foreign to him because he had been raised in such a harsh environment. His thoughts had taken on the voice of his critical mother. To this day, unconditional self-acceptance is still a work in progress for him.

All of us are beautiful, imperfect works in progress.

MANY OF MY PAST CLIENTS have struggled with viewing imperfections as personal deficits rather than important pieces to their complicated lives. One particular client, Deb, an honors student in college, once barely passed a statistics class. During this particular semester, her grandfather, with whom she was close, passed away and Deb had to miss a few days of school. She grumbled that she was such a failure because everyone expected her to always make perfect grades, and she had always lived up to that expectation. The lowest final grade that she had ever made in school was a B-, which did not please her.

I encouraged her to be aware of what is called *all-or-nothing thinking*. It is an erroneous form of thinking that does not allow an in-between, gray area. This is not how life operates. Life is filled with gray. Deb thought in black and white, 'If I make all A's, I'm smart or if I make a B, I'm dumb.' I informed her that most people have said mean things before, but that doesn't define them as mean people. They have probably said nice things, but that doesn't necessarily make them a nice person. Hold labels and judgments about yourself gently and lightly. Be mindful and intentional about labeling behaviors, not people. If you must define yourself, would you be willing to define yourself as an imperfect human? Be mindful that you can make mistakes and still be smart, kind, and loving.

Freedom from pleasing others

JOHN LYDGATE, author of *The Temple of Glas*, said, 'You can please some of the people all the time, you can please all the people some of the time, but you can't please all the people all the time.'

SUMMER ADMITS THAT SHE ALWAYS WANTS to make other people happy. She's non-confrontational because she doesn't want to rock the boat and cause confusion. She is passive-aggressive because she doesn't want to deal with situations head-on.

Summer was a skinny child and always teased by her family and friends. As an adult, she entered a relationship and her partner teased her about being skinny. She really wanted to make him happy, so she gained weight and became overweight. People from her childhood could barely notice her.

When Summer gained weight, people, including her partner, continued teasing her. Everybody asked why she would gain so much weight. People teased her even more because of the contrast from extremely thin to extremely large. Summer was just as unhappy heavy as she was skinny. She thought, *'I'm damned if I do, and I'm damned if I don't'* play the people pleasing game.

People will always find something critical to say about you. Happiness will remain elusive until you are free from the prison of being dependent on what other people think. You can't please them all, so why not please yourself by doing what matters and is important to you?

One of the main barriers to self-acceptance is caring too much about what other people will think about you.

I SUGGEST YOU PRACTICE the skill of doing what is important to you despite what others may think. One way to practice getting over the hump of over-focusing on what others may think is to intentionally engage in behaviors that you know will attract disapproval.

- Wear mismatched clothes or don't comb your hair when you leave the house.
- Ask for support the next time you are struggling, even if you prize your independence.
- Ask a question in a situation where you otherwise would not because you don't want people to think you are unintelligent.

SUCCESSFUL PEOPLE ARE COURAGEOUS and take calculated risks. It takes courage to stand up for your beliefs and risk being judged, criticized, and evaluated. Ordinary people become successful when they stop focusing on the approval of others.

To some degree, it is understandable that we care what other people think. We are social beings. Most of us have been socialized to care about the approval of others, starting with the approval or our parents. As a 10-year-old, you might have wanted to wear mismatched clothes to school that were appropriate to the season. There is a high probability that your parent tried to change your mind about it. Why? Your parent likely worried that other people might think she was a tacky, tasteless, bad parent.

There are probably many examples throughout your life where you were rewarded for conforming to social norms. Our human species cares more about what other humans think about us than what we think about our Selves. This is why we can benefit from tapping into our Best Self that is free from the approval of others. When we reclaim ourselves, we can flexibly wear diverse mental hats and not lose ourselves in worrying about what other people think of us.

Our need of approval from others is ancient. According to evolutionary psychology, early humans had to learn how to fit into groups, meet the approval of others, and cooperate in order to survive. Our minds naturally send information to us to help us fit in with groups, meet the approval of others, care about what others think, and most importantly, survive.

It is difficult to shake the overwhelming desire to care about what other people think.

WE MIGHT NOT BE ABLE TO CHANGE whether we care about someone's approval of us, but we can change our behavior. If we are to live the life of our choosing, not the life that someone else ascribes to us, we will need to know when to behave based upon what someone thinks and when not to behave based on what other people think.

There are times when it is necessary to care about what other people think, especially people who matter. It makes sense, some of the time, for you to want to please your partner and care what she thinks. Be mindful that you can lose yourself if you attempt to please your partner all the time. You will need to be aware of your own needs and intentional about expressing them and getting them met.

What difference does it make if an acquaintance at work makes an off-handed comment about your outfit? Your colleague says, in a playful, yet somewhat patronizing way, 'You are awfully colorful today.' What if this comment occurred in the morning, and you find it difficult to concentrate for the remainder of the day? You keep replaying the words *awfully colorful.* What did she mean by awfully colorful? Do I look awful? Is colorful good or bad? Interestingly, this comment will have more of an impact if you have mental knots around the theme of wanting to meet the approval of others. If you do not place a lot of value on what you wear and what other people think, then this comment might have less impact on you.

Humorous questions to ask yourself if you find that you are ruminating about the comment include, 'Does this person pay my bills?' and 'Would this person's approval get me somewhere significant in life?' If the answer is no to both questions, then it will be helpful to not take the comments of this person seriously or personally. A serious question to ask yourself is, 'Why am I prone to being annoyed by these types of comments?'

The comment was made, and there is nothing that could be done about what has already happened. There are several things that you can do to reclaim your Best Self in this situation.

- Practice letting go of the attachment to the comment by noticing the words that are causing you pain (awfully colorful), and then trying the suggestions that might take the sting away and lessen the impact.
- Try to find the humor in the words.
- Write the words down to notice that they are just letters that can't hurt you.
- Say the words in a funny voice.

The point is to do what you need to do in order to be able to move forward throughout your day without being drained by trying to evaluate a comment that someone made. If it makes the situation any better, the other person probably made the comment because of her own difficulty and insecurity about her appearance. She could have projected her own issues onto you. It is up to you whether you choose to accept her issues as your own.

'I've learned that you shouldn't go through life with a catcher's mitt on both hands; you need to be able to throw something back.'
— Maya Angelou

PRACTICE SEEING THE BIGGER PICTURE. In the grand scheme of your life, what difference does an off-hand comment make when you have bigger fish to fry? If you don't have more important things going on in your life that are bigger than an off-hand comment, then you might need to get some real business.

What if, instead of a colleague making a comment about your attire, your boss said that you are looking awfully colorful today? Then, given that this person matters, you may want to put some energy into considering the situation in which the comment occurred and maybe talking to a friend about the comment. What I do not want to imply is that you spend a significant amount of time in your head trying to figure out what someone meant, even your boss. It wouldn't hurt to ask your boss if your outfit is appropriate so that you can make an informed decision. I am not implying that you need to comply. I'm just suggesting that you gather information as you make wise and effective decisions.

Given that your boss made a comment about your attire, this is where it is necessary to use your experience to help inform behavior. Is this the first time that someone has commented on your attire in the workplace? What exactly were you wearing? Was it appropriate to the setting? If you are unsure, ask a friend. Other mindful questions to ask yourself include:

- Does there appear to be a clothing norm in this agency?
- Do I value this job?
- Do I want to be promoted?

ONE'S APPEARANCE *SHOULD* NOT MATTER when it comes to promotion and upward mobility, but in some cases, it does. It is what it is! Mindful Acceptance encourages us to be aware of the social and cultural contexts and intentional about how we choose to deal with them. It is your choice how to behave in these situations. Just know that society doesn't always conform to what we think *should* occur. You are reclaiming your Best Self when you behave in ways that demonstrate that you don't care about things that don't matter.

*'The art of being wise is
the art of knowing what to overlook.'*
— *William James*

IT IS VERY DIFFICULT to make yourself stop caring about something. Have you ever been in an unhealthy relationship and couldn't make yourself stop loving your partner? Instead of trying to control your innate response of caring, you could shift your attention to focusing on things that are helpful for you to care about. If you have an intentional, *I don't care, so what, and no big deal* attitude about things that don't really matter, then you won't give excessive attention to unimportant matters. The cognitive energy being applied to things that are insignificant can be better used when transformed into actions that matter.

One way to unhook from being caught up in giving too much attention to what someone else thinks is to practice not taking yourself, others, or the world so seriously. Everything isn't of earth shattering importance. Laugh at your Self from time to time. Envision your Self as a fly on the wall observing some of the thoughts that you get wrapped up in and give yourself permission to laugh hysterically.

Self-acceptance in action

ONCE WE ARE COMFORTABLE and confident in our own skin, we are not easily moved by external factors, such as the behavior of others and our circumstances. Unconditional self-acceptance can stand alone as the hidden jewel to life satisfaction, *and it is accessible to everyone.*

Unconditional self-acceptance is the intentional and active engagement in thoughts and behaviors that directly enhance our relationship with our Best Self. It unlocks and enables self-love, self-esteem, and self-worth. Unconditional self-acceptance is an awareness of ourselves that is unrelenting and without conditions. Unconditional self-acceptance means we are open and curious about every aspect of ourselves, *no matter what,* including the good, the bad, and the ugly. Additionally, unconditional self-acceptance allows us to be receptive to the awareness of who we are and what life has to offer at any given time without getting stuck in storylines that prevent us from engaging in meaningful behavior. Unconditional self-acceptance is so powerful that I believe it is the prerequisite for self-growth and self-enhancement.

*Unconditional self-acceptance means we are open and
curious about every aspect of ourselves, no matter what,
including the good, the bad, and the ugly.*

MANY RESEARCHERS DESCRIBE self-acceptance as an attitude.
Unconditional self-acceptance takes self-acceptance a step further and describes it as an active way of dealing with ourselves,
others, and the world. So, yes, it is an attitude, but it is also a
skill that produces intentional behaviors. It might be helpful
to select some coping statements that facilitate Mindful Acceptance of ourselves, others, relationships, and the world. A
few coping statements that I use for myself and that clients
often find helpful include:

- It is what it is.
- I can't change what has already happened.
- Let go and let God.
- Anxious thoughts are normal.
- Pain is inevitable, suffering is optional.

COPING STATEMENTS ARE NOT INTENDED to erase your current intrusive thoughts about yourself, your past, your situation, others, or the world. There is nothing that can magically

stop your mind from telling you mean, nasty, scary, hurtful, and unhelpful things. Once you are able to find some distance between your Self and your thoughts by noticing them, then you are able to be intentional and creative about planting other thought 'seeds' that might motivate you to engage in life enhancing and worthwhile behaviors.

Don't wait to feel courageous; begin engaging in daily courageous acts and see what happens.

THE MORE WE ENGAGE in courageous behaviors, the more we are able to strengthen the belief that we are courageous. The more we try new behaviors and explore outside our comfort zones, the greater our chances of taking our life situations to another level.

People think of large-scale heroic acts as courageous. Martin Luther King Jr., Rosa Parks, and Mahatma Gandhi are all honored heroes. However, courage doesn't have to exist on such a large scale; it can be found in everyday acts. Two popular terms for this type of courage are everyday courage and ordinary courage. For some people, just getting out of bed, when depressed and anxious, and going to work could be considered courageous. For others, raising your hand at a meeting could be courageous.

Courage can be seen in behaving the opposite of your default behavior. If you are prone to avoiding emotionally arousing situations, confronting the situation might be considered courageous for you. Be mindful that the opposite is considered courageous. If you are prone to 'popping off' and confronting every situation head on, it might be courageous for you to allow anxious energy to flow through you without acting on it. Consider what is courageous for you and commit to engaging in some courageous acts. Don't wait to feel courageous; begin engaging in daily courageous acts and see what happens. Ask yourself, 'What does courage look like for me today?'

Genuine self-love

GENUINE SELF-LOVE MEANS that you accept that at this very moment, you are who you are, insecurities and all. You feel what you feel. Your genetic makeup is your genetic makeup. Your culture is your culture. When you truly accept your inner Self, you will be showing love to yourself. Can you imagine the turmoil in loving half of who you are and hating or attempting to disregard the other half? That will set you up to search for your complete Self in other people and sometimes dangerous external sources.

When you do not love all of yourself, you feel lost and incomplete, which explains the search for happiness outside yourself. However, when you fully love yourself, you are able to tap into all your internal resources and feel complete with or without other external sources. Genuine self-love means people, places, and things will be ancillary, and you will not feel like your world is ending when they change or leave.

You are in a healthy space when you *want* other people to be in your life, but do not *need* them. Most people feel lost when they think that they are missing something or somebody that they *need* for survival. I would suggest that what you *need* is an integrated relationship with your whole Self and your higher power, however you choose to define it. In order to prevent feeling strong attachments that seem to threaten your survival, begin to adopt the intentional statement, 'I'm good with or without x, y, or z.' Don't stop with the intentional statement. When you find yourself losing whatever you are attached to, begin engaging in behaviors that demonstrate that you love yourself, regardless.

We can fully love ourselves right now, today, bringing our entire messy masterpiece into awareness, increasing compassion about our mess, and engaging in intentional and creative decisions that honor our entire Self. Self-loving behaviors could include: engaging in a hobby (cooking, sewing, reading, writing, exercising), learning something new, earning a degree, or meeting new people. How can you show love to your Self?

Becoming whole

WE HAVE TO ALLOW ALL the feelings and thoughts that are occurring in this very moment to flow and be at peace with all that is occurring within us. If we are able to perceive our thoughts as fleeting images and symbols and emotions as transient energy, then we might be less likely to become trapped by them.

Internal fighting and segregating good thoughts/emotions from bad thoughts/emotions will only breed more internal conflict, which could prevent us from behaving in ways consistent with our Best Self. The solution to internal discord is to remember that you are the observer of the internal activity and that you are free to choose where you focus your attention and how you behave.

Human suffering languishes in the gap between what we have and what we want, who we are and who we want to be, what we can and what we cannot change, and the resistance to 'what is.'

YOUR SELF IS the guardian and watcher of all that occurs within you. Suffering ceases and happiness flourishes when we return to a place of wholeness.

For instance, Sally has a history of being addicted to alcohol. She may spend a great deal of time resisting the fact that she has sensitivity to alcohol. Sally may feel annoyed that she can't drink socially without getting drunk. It's useless for her to spend a lot of time feeling sad and ruminating about how life would have been so different if she didn't have that sensitivity. Mindful Acceptance offers Sally freedom from her struggle with reality and the resulting sadness and unproductive behaviors.

Don't judge, label, or analyze the struggle. Just know that the struggle is real and notice it. Upon noticing it, take a few gentle breaths, and make psychological space for *sitting with* the reality of your current struggle. The unfortunate reality isn't going anywhere, so it's better to simply make room for the sadness of it and go on about the business of living a life that is sober, meaningful, and worthwhile.

If both of your parents had diabetes, you would be considered at-risk for developing diabetes. You might struggle with this reality by constantly comparing yourself to people who appear to eat whatever they want. You might continually think about what you *should* be able to do, and get stuck in wishful thinking about how life would look if you were not at-risk.

There is no good reason to experience undue suffering. The predisposition to diabetes could be nothing more than a predisposition to diabetes. Being angry and irritated about our reality will not change the reality. *It is what it is!* We can choose to accept that we have a predisposition to diabetes while refusing to waste any time or energy wishing that we did not have it. We can become willing to accept that we were made this way for a reason beyond our current awareness. No longer do we have to expend energy on a moot cause. We are empowered to choose to put our energy to good use in areas where we can affect change.

One thing that we cannot change is our history. If you appear to have a predisposition to intense anxiety, you can certainly take steps to keep the anxiety manageable, but you cannot change what happened in childhood, which is that you learned a certain response pattern to your stream of thoughts. You can absolutely work on changing how you respond to your thoughts.

You will benefit greatly by refusing to waste any more time or energy wishing that you did not experience anxiety or worrying about worrying. It will not be helpful to chastise yourself for not being able to relax your mind the way that other people *appear* to relax their minds. We become anxious about anxiety. We squander a lot of precious time fantasizing about how life could have been different if we didn't experience anxiety. This vicious cycle will continue to repeat itself until we become aware of the patterns.

If you have a predisposition to 'big bones' and 'thickness,' there is nothing that you can do about the fact that your family has big bones. However, you can surely take steps to keep the weight at bay or manage it. Predispositions don't dictate outcome. Your behavior determines outcome.

'Don't compare your life to others.
There's no comparison between the sun and the moon.
They shine when it's their time.'
— Anonymous proverb

LET'S NOT BEAT OURSELVES UP for our genetics and not being able to eat things that other people appear to be able to eat or do things that other people appear to be able to do. Comparison is self-defeating, punitive, and sometimes downright mean. Comparing ourselves to others who appear to have what we want will not do us any good. Even comparing ourselves to our idealized Self is dangerous. We never truly know when it will be our time to shine. Stop comparing and start embracing behaviors that encourage you to be your Best Self, no matter what. If we are mindful of our predispositions, we can avoid undue suffering.

We can be creative about thinking thoughts that support our awareness of the predisposition, intentional about practicing coping statements and mindfulness activities, and self-compassionate during the times when we deny our current reality. Predispositions will be nothing more than predispositions. It is what it is!

I KINDLY REMINDED EMILY, who was struggling with intense anxiety, 'You don't want it; why would you? But you have it, now what are we going to do about it?' We all deal with an internal voice that has a lot to say about a lot of things. Emily just wanted her anxiety to go away, yet she wasn't ready to open up to it, make room for it, or sit with it. I shared an amazing and powerful poem with Emily by a poet, Jae Nichelle called 'Friends with Benefits.' This incredibly popular poem candidly and humorously depicts her relationship with her anxiety. She opens up by saying:

> *So, my anxiety and I have what some people might call a friends with benefits relationship. We have no love for each other, but she still just like f*%@s with me sometimes, ya know?*

The poem closes with:

> *I think the reason my relationships don't work out is because no one knows they're signing up for a threesome. I understand, I know how hard it is to live with both of us when we don't like feeling out of control, when we don't handle conflict well, when we don't handle being yelled at well, when everything you say to us will be repeated and deconstructed and analyzed in our head a million times after, and if I am silent for a while...it is because I have to fight with her before I can fight with you. I've tried to cut her off before. I cannot. We do not handle separation well because of our parents, I mean our ex, I mean our friends, breathe, so I guess my anxiety and I have just learned to live together. She's the longest relationship I have ever had and as everyone leaves she is the only relationship that I can count on.*

This poem resonates with Emily and many of my other clients. Emily eventually learned to notice that it wasn't her anxiety that was problematic, but how she dealt with her thoughts and bodily sensations, which we call anxiety. Slowly, Emily began to open up to the possibility that she could lessen the impact that anxiety was having on her life by learning to lean into it instead of resisting it.

Intentional thoughts that might help someone struggling with intense anxiety include:

- This is just a thought made up of letters, words, and symbols that cannot hurt me.
- This thought and feeling will pass.
- I am the observer, watcher, and noticer of my thought.

We can make lasting changes after we mindfully accept what we are resisting and make psychological room for 'that which is.' Mindful Acceptance simply means that we are not resisting what is beyond our power to change; instead, we are empowering ourselves to change what we can.

Raw realness

THERE ARE SOME ASPECTS of your reality that you do not have the power to change, such as what has already occurred in the past, other people's behavior, some of your unwelcome thoughts, and initial reactions. However, you do have the power to change many relevant parts of your reality. You can change jobs, relationships, commitments, and some aspects of your appearance.

The first step toward changing what is within your power to change is to be mindful and acknowledge what the reality is right *now*. It will not be helpful to minimize, sugar coat, or dilute your reality. The more raw and honest you are with yourself, the better equipped you will be at making lasting changes. You will need to be intentional and creative about changing your reality in ways that make sense for your life, not your neighbor's life, but *your* life!

Are you willing to take a minute and be real about your reality by noticing what your mind is telling you right now as you consider 'being real?' If so, do not judge what your mind is telling you at this present moment. Just allow the thoughts to come and go like people on the busy streets of New York City. As you allow your thoughts to come and go, pause, and gently notice your breath. Air will enter your nostrils, fill up in your lungs, and gently exit your mouth. Take a minute and just notice. During this process, your mind naturally pulls you away from the present moment. That is normal. Thank your mind for doing its job, become self-compassionate for whatever thoughts were brought to your attention, and commit to engaging in a life that is full of meaning and purpose.

Embracing your Best Self

OUR SEXUALITY may not be under our control. Most older generations were taught that people were supposed to be attracted to the opposite sex. Religion was used to substantiate this idea, sometimes with great brutality. Because of this approach, many people grew up being taught one way but feeling the total opposite. This might explain why we had so many people who were 'in the closet' and living double lives for so many years.

Interestingly, I had a past client, Roy, an older gentleman who had been married for over 30 years. He always knew that he was attracted to males. Nevertheless, he did what his family and society told him to do, which was to attempt to like girls, date girls, get married to a woman, and have children. Unfortunately, he never felt fulfilled in his marriage or life. He always felt that he was betraying his true Self by marrying a woman. Acknowledging his attraction to men to himself or anyone else was not an option for him growing up during the 1950's.

Roy's family was clear about how they felt about homosexuality, and he did not want to be disowned and shunned. He described himself as being a depressed adolescent who grew up to become a depressed adult. Roy hated himself because he could not understand why he couldn't turn off his attraction to men. For a long time, Roy just wanted to be 'normal' and do what was expected of him.

Roy had numerous same-sex affairs and one-night stands with men while he was married, which he hated himself for doing. His wife never found out. There was suspicion but never confirmation. Roy's wife passed a couple years ago, at which time Roy decided to come completely out of the closet. His coming out prompted him to visit me so that he could have a safe, non-judgmental environment in which to explore his sexual orientation. Roy was done with being a 'good boy' and doing things to make other people feel comfortable. He was ready to accept himself and live in his truth. Who am I, or anyone else to dispute his personal truth? I encourage you to be true to your inner Self as long as you are living a life of your choosing and not harming other humans or life forms. It's far more dangerous to deny our reality than to live within it.

Everyone has been forced to deny certain aspects of themselves at one point or another. For instance, when Sam was little boy, his father warned him not to cry. Sam wasn't allowed to be sensitive in his environment because girls were considered sensitive. As an adult, he neglects his feminine aspects. Everyone has both feminine and masculine characteristics. We function at our best when we are cultivating all our power within.

Diane was told not to play with trucks because trucks were for boys. What if she sincerely enjoyed playing with trucks? The truck-playing part of her development was suppressed so that she could exist in her environment. This part of her personality never truly goes away; it may remain dormant until the environment is ripe for expression.

I had a client whose mother would swat his hand with a switch every time that he would attempt to use his left hand.

This situation was traumatic and set him up to deny aspects of himself in order to make other people feel comfortable, while neglecting his own comfort and Self.

Some people were forced to deny aspects of themselves more severely than others. As a powerful expression of self-care, I encourage you to get in touch with your whole Self and acknowledge all its parts. Stop suppressing and embrace your Best Self. Be true to your Self while acknowledging that you share this world with other people.

Keeping it 100

YOU WILL MOVE AROUND IN THE WORLD SKILLFULLY and purposefully when you are 100% real with yourself. Mindful Acceptance helps you become best friends with your Self. You are the only person that will always be there for your Self; don't be phony with your most powerful ally. Once you are aware of who you are, then you can be intentional about deciding who has earned the privilege of meeting all of you. I am so grateful and appreciative to all my clients who have been brave enough to be real and share their stories with me. It takes a lot of courage to open up to another human.

Opening up and sharing one's Self with the right person at the right time is cathartic, therapeutic, and invigorating. Sharing your true story can lead you to feeling energized because you are releasing the tension of holding on tightly to information that you might have been protecting for a long time.

The reason that many people seek licensed therapists is because they are aware that most people aren't naturally nonjudgmental and validating. Humans are naturally judgmental and critical. Most people, especially people with whom you are close, have a lot to say about your situation because they feel that they know what is best for you. These people mean well and care about you. It's just that their method of trying to help, often times, just doesn't help. They will want to take away your pain immediately. They might say something like, 'You *shouldn't* feel that way.' However, what most people need when they are being vulnerable and sharing their story is someone who has good listening and validating skills and is able to sit with the pain that you are so courageously sharing.

Be mindful and intentional about to whom and what you choose to share of yourself. Unconditional self-acceptance means that you are aware of your strengths and limitations. It has nothing to do with sharing your strengths and limitations with everybody you meet. One of the worst things that can happen to you when you make your Self vulnerable by sharing your story is for the receiver of information to personalize what is being heard, especially if the situation has nothing to do with her. The human experience is so complex that we can barely handle our own truths, much less have the compassion and empathy to understand the truths of others. This is one reason why we struggle with being truly intimate with a large amount of people.

Just because you are not 100% real with someone doesn't mean that you are not being yourself. It just means that you are not exposing all of yourself to someone you cannot trust with your vulnerabilities. How much of yourself you choose to reveal to certain people is entirely your choice.

Being the real you

UNDERNEATH THE MANY FAÇADES that we use to survive, everyone has an inborn biological temperament that affects thoughts, behaviors, and emotions. Many of us were raised in environments that did not appreciate our temperament. We can say that our temperament did not fit with our environment or our environment did not accommodate our temperament. The *goodness of fit* concept is the match or mismatch between our temperament and environment.

When a mismatch of the environment occurred, many of us had to learn to perfect the art of identifying with mental representations or egos, which are façades and shields that help us survive in our environments. If Susan had high emotional reactivity as a child, but her primary caregivers struggled with tolerating emotions, her caregivers might have shunned, teased, or ignored her for displaying emotions. Susan might have had to create a mental representation to show that she was not prone to emotional reactions. People might have begun to see Susan as emotionless, which was far from the truth. Because of this environmental mismatch, she might have begun to bottle up her emotions until she couldn't keep up the charade anymore, resulting in explosive breakdowns.

In children, this might look like a child with a behavior disturbance. In adults, this might appear as frequent physical manifestations of your emotional world, such as coming down with the flu or experiencing recurrent migraines. It's hard work to behave in a way that is incongruent with your natural disposition.

The practice of the four disciples of Mindful Acceptance will help you increase awareness of some of your ineffective behaviors. Awareness and a commitment to what is most important in life will empower you to make better decisions.

A VERY LOVELY past female client of mine, Taki, was raised in an emotionally abusive environment. Her mother was chronically depressed, neglectful, and emotionally withdrawn. Taki was not taught how to show love toward herself or others. She didn't know how it felt to experience love. She began to look for love outside the home. She said and did whatever it took to be accepted and loved. She did not truly accept herself, which made it difficult for her to fully accept a partner. Her lack of self-acceptance made her judgmental and critical of herself and her partner. Because she so deeply wanted to be accepted and loved, she often didn't address her wants and needs with other people. Taki's issues with her partner would build up, but she would not assert herself. Instead, she would internalize her problems and become more depressed and withdrawn.

I encouraged Taki to practice self-compassion with her tendency to engage in attention-seeking and self-destructive behaviors. She began to notice when her mind was being judgmental and critical for past thoughts and actions. Taki become aware of and acknowledged her tendencies by noticing when her thoughts and emotions were getting in the way of asserting herself and engaging in behavior based upon her values. She became intentional and creative about choosing value-driven thoughts and behaviors to guide her on her life journey. When Taki engaged in self-destructive behaviors, she reminded herself that she can't change what has already happened, but she can attempt to make a different decision the next time a situation occurs that triggers her to engage in unhelpful behaviors. Becoming aware of your triggers is a crucial step towards intentional and creative behavior. We want to learn to act based upon our values and not act exclusively to get rid of unwanted emotions or thoughts.

Intentional belonging

WE CANNOT CHANGE the environments into which we were born, but as adults, we have the power to choose which career and personal environments are the best fits for us. I was raised as an only child. I did not have to compete for love, attention, or favor from my primary caregivers. As a child, I did not spend time with large groups of people for extended periods of time. I've always enjoyed being around other people, but in small, intimate settings.

As a child, I did not know why I gravitated towards smaller groups; what I did know was that I felt I belonged in smaller settings. I didn't have to behave out of character or put on a show to belong in smaller groups, which I might have had to do to fit into larger groups.

Brené Brown explores the difference between fitting in and belonging in *The Gifts of Imperfection*. She informs us that attempting to fit in gets in the way of belonging. I define 'fitting in' as a molding, bending, and flexing of your personality so that you can be accepted. While trying to fit in, you are trying to prove your worthiness to be accepted. Belonging is being exactly who you are and knowing that you are accepted and loved. I am glad that I did not try to become someone that I wasn't by trying to fit in with large groups rather than being myself where I belonged in small, intimate settings.

YOU WILL BE MUCH HAPPIER if your career choice fits your personality. Are you doing what you truly enjoy or what someone said you *should* do? Increase your connectedness with your life purpose. You will know when you are living in your purpose because you will not have to struggle to fit in; you will know deep in your soul that you are where you belong.

I was discouraged from going into the field of psychology as an undergraduate student. I was asked if I knew of anyone who looked like me in the field. My answer was, 'No.' I was asked if I knew exactly what I would do with a psychology degree, and at that time, my answer was, 'No.' I allowed others to influence my decision because I decided to take a major in business marketing with a minor in psychology. Admittedly, I was scared of making a poor career decision. I was the first person on my father's side of the family to complete college, so there was a lot of pressure on me to *prove* that it made sense to obtain a degree. At that time in my life, I still felt that I needed to prove myself to other people.

I have increased awareness of my human desire to prove myself and have distanced my Self from thoughts that are not helpful. Disentanglement from my unhealthy thoughts equipped me to make decisions that are intentional and aligned with my values. Today, I am aware of when I feel the need to prove myself, and I can be intentional about managing my behaviors.

Thankfully, I did not give up on my dreams, and I encourage you not to give up on yours. I decided to take as many undergraduate psychology courses as possible, intern, and work in the clinical field. During my senior year of undergraduate school, I applied for entrance into doctoral programs, and I was accepted into Roosevelt University in Chicago. I continued to pursue my dreams, and the rest is history!

I encourage you to accept unconditionally and unapologetically, without judgment, everything about your Self, including the automatic thoughts, emotions, and behaviors that have not always worked for you in the past. Stop apologizing and making excuses for accepting and loving your Self! Be mindful, intentional, and self-compassionate as you navigate through life.

Best Self in Action: Self-acceptance

UNCONDITIONAL SELF-ACCEPTANCE BEGINS with an open, curious, and flexible posture towards your Self. Allow the questions below to help you become more aware of your internal world and how you relate to your Self.

- Do you become defensive when people mention your less than positive traits?
- Are you preoccupied with what other people will think about you?
- Do you struggle with trying to change the apparent fact that you have certain sensitivities that other people don't have, such as to alcohol or sugar?
- Are you spending a lot of time trying to figure out *why* you can't be like everybody else?
- Do you ever wish that you were someone else?

If you answered yes to any of the above questions or know that there are things about your Self that you refuse to accept, especially specific thoughts and emotions, then you are resisting the reality of something about your Self. You can learn to behave as your Best Self and stop resisting what is happening in your internal world. Create what you want in your physical world. Refuse to resist what you cannot control.

Part 2

BETTER, MORE FULFULLING RELATIOINSHIPS

WHY DO SOME PEOPLE become so angry when they get cut off in traffic? Some people really do think that other drivers are out to get them and are purposefully trying to make them late. If so, this thought is the furthest from the truth. Quite frankly, the driver would have cut anyone off to get to his destination. To avoid getting swept away by anger and frustration, it is helpful to be mindful that certain situations have absolutely nothing to do with you. We cannot control our initial emotions, but we can control our behaviors. We can embrace the liberating truth that most situations are not about us. Try pausing, breathing, and letting go of trying to change what has already happened. Most importantly, practice self-compassion, especially if you did not handle a situation the way you would have liked.

9

DON'T MAKE IT PERSONAL

T HE EGO IS OFTEN THOUGHT OF as the aspect of the personality that is vulnerable and thinks that everything is about us. The ego is a metaphor, stemming from the *thinking self*, similar to the inner child. It can be thought of as the sensitive and vulnerable part of our personality that we feel the need to defend and protect, sometimes at all costs. Thoughts that are ego-inspired can incite anger, mistrust, personalization, comparisons, and jealousy.

Don Miguel Ruiz, in *The Four Agreements*, informs us to not take anything personally because what happens to us is not about us but more about something that is out of our control. Most of the time, we are so consumed with our inner thoughts about our own problems that we are not thinking about other people, and other people are not thinking about us. Be mindful of taking things personally that are not meant for you. Don't take ownership of something that is not yours to own, such as other people's mental knots and behaviors.

Interpersonal relationships are complicated. It is hard to know what another person is thinking, why they behaved a certain way, and what is going on in her life. Harper's friend, Morgan, doesn't text her back immediately. Harper's mind tells her that Morgan is ignoring her, doesn't like her, and doesn't want to talk to her anymore. These intrusive thoughts are perfectly normal. It becomes problematic if Harper *believes* these thoughts. She would then be causing herself to suffer unnecessarily because she had not accepted that the situation might not have been about her at all. Morgan might be struggling with a family emergency.

SUSIE'S MOTHER, FRANCIS, is negative and judgmental. As hard as this may seem, it would be wise for Susie to not take her mother's words personally. Francis may have unresolved issues that need to be addressed and mental knots that need to be untied. Susie would benefit from not allowing Francis's criticisms to set up shop in her mental landscape. Susie can achieve this by limiting how much mental energy she invests into thinking *why* Francis treats her the way she does or why Francis behaves a particular way. Susie may benefit more from using the same energy that annoyed her about Francis's behavior to self-soothe and untie her own knots by compassionately asking herself why does Francis's criticisms bother her as much as they do. Susie would feel much better and engage more effectively with the world if she focuses on healing her own wounds rather than trying to figure out Francis's issues.

One of the ways to take the sting away from words is to change their context. Some intrusive thoughts are like mental seeds that others have planted. We can replant those thoughts in new gardens, given that we can't get rid of the intrusive thoughts. In Susie's situation, she can consciously imagine her mother's words as floating by on a cloud in the sky or floundering along a bank as a leaf in a stream. Susie can change the context of Francis's words by writing the words on a piece of paper and noticing that the words are just words.

Susie can be intentional about thinking, 'Don't take it personally: accept the reality of her critical behavior and govern yourself accordingly.' Susie can live her life without allowing Francis's words to get in the way. For Susie, it is helpful for her to be creative and remember that she has options. As an adult, she can choose where and with whom she would like to spend her time.

Don't Make it Personal

Have you ever had difficulty with a friend who took things personally that were not meant for her? For example, Stephanie confided in her longtime friend Anya about her romantic partner being cheap. Anya responded, 'I bet you think I'm cheap because I don't purchase name brand clothes and shoes.' Anya's mind was in overdrive and Anya did not appear to be the driver. Stephanie would explain she did not think that Anya was cheap and that she would never say that about her.

Stephanie rarely felt heard when she conversed with Anya because Anya frequently made the situation about her. As a result of this type of behavior, Stephanie began limiting what type of conversations she would have with Anya. It would be helpful for Stephanie to communicate with her friend the next time that this type of personalizing occurred and give Anya the opportunity to correct her behavior. Stephanie needs to be mindful that she cannot change Anya's behavior. She can influence Anya's behavior by communicating her needs and setting boundaries, even if that means spending less time together.

For Stephanie to be able to set these types of boundaries, she will have to learn to weather through Anya's reactions. Anya might provide an angry or hurt response. Regardless,

Stephanie will have to courageously stand her ground and deflect Anya's reactions that might try to guilt Stephanie into loosening her boundaries.

You are entitled to stand up for your beliefs, rights, boundaries, and Self. Be mindful that for every action there is a reaction. Just because you think you are doing something honorable by asserting yourself, that doesn't mean it will be without reactions.

Be courageous enough to deal with the resulting consequences. Just as you are entitled to assert yourself, so is everyone else in the world. Be intentional about behaving in ways that are consistent with your chosen values. Be mindful of whether your chosen values are helping you Behave as your Best Self. If your values are not leading you in the direction that you want your life to go, then become intentional about changing them. They are your values to pick and choose.

There is great power in choosing when
to take things personally.

PEOPLE BEHAVE A CERTAIN WAY because of their own issues and insecurities, not necessarily because of anything that others have done. Bosses may be rude because of their own issues, not because they are out to get specific people, so it doesn't make sense to take their behavior personally.

The Self on social media

JIM AND HIS BUDDY RALPH were in conflict about a business relationship that was going bad. Initially, they had each invested a substantial amount of money, time, and effort. Ralph felt that Jim had recently started slacking on his commitment to projects and increasing revenue opportunities. Coincidentally or not, Ralph posted a message on social media stating, 'Success and greatness only comes to those who are committed and work hard.' Jim's ego told him that the message was meant for him and that he needed to defend himself. The posting may or may not have been meant for Jim. If Ralph wasn't brave enough to address the message directly to Jim, then Jim may want to consider not taking the message personally.

After re-reading the post, Jim noticed his own personalizing, and refused to put energy into trying to figure out if the post was a direct attack on him. Instead, he became intentional about thinking, 'This message was not addressed to me; therefore, I will not accept it as for me.' Jim committed to engaging in behaviors that were important to him, such as figuring out ways to dissolve his current business amicably with Ralph and determining how to create a new business venture without him. If a social media post is not directly addressed to you, don't accept it as belonging to you.

Social media wars can be brutal. Be mindful that once you type something in the social medium, you cannot get it back. It is on display for the entire world to see. I've seen lovers broadcast all their dirty laundry online for the world to judge, scrutinize, and ridicule. Look at Stevie J and Joseline from *Love and Hip Hop Atlanta*. Their situation is a hot mess for all the world to see.

Many people live vicariously through the lives of others who post all their business online. Be mindful if you are providing free entertainment for others. Don't allow defending your ego to get you in a social media mess.

Eliminating unhealthy pride

FOOLISH PRIDE IS an inflated sense of self-worth that overcompensates for low self-worth. The world doesn't revolve around our foolish pride, so the risk of our pride being offended is high.

People with a lot of prideful thoughts often seem aggressive and unemotional. However, they are full of emotions, just not the warm and fuzzy ones. They are typically very emotional beings that are versed in expressing anger, but they struggle with expressing sad and hurt emotions.

Foolish pride causes irrational and unrealistic behavior that can strain relationships.

SOMEONE WITH PRIDEFUL THOUGHTS may think that if you don't return their call, you are being extremely disrespectful. Or, if you are occasionally late, that you are personally attacking them and wasting their time. The anger and frustration for the perceived level of disrespect can be wildly out of proportion. It will be challenging for the two people to see eye-to-eye given the probable irrational perspective of the person indulging in foolish pride.

Pride can make people behave in ways that appear out of character. If an individual perceives that someone has wronged him, then prideful thoughts may lead the person to engage in unhealthy behavior. If a man entertains thoughts that his wife doesn't give him the attention that he deserves, prideful thoughts may justify him to step outside the relationship.

Be mindful of prideful thoughts and intentional about not acting on them if they are not leading you in the direction of what's most important, such as meaningful relationships, a successful career, or health and wellness.

I ONCE WORKED WITH KATE AND MIKE, a couple in their early twenties. The presenting concern was possible infidelity between Mike and a receptionist, Linda, who worked at a call center. Kate worked in corporate America, while Mike was a blue-collar worker. Kate made significantly more money than Mike.

Who makes the most money *shouldn't* matter, right? Hmm. Well, let's see.

Mike initiated the call to schedule an appointment. I was surprised because in a male/female relationship, typically the female calls to make the initial appointment. Most times, but not always, the partner who initiates contact is usually the partner most motivated to begin counseling and secretly wants the other person to change. In this situation, Mike called because he was in the doghouse and he was willing to do whatever it took to get out.

During our couple's sessions, Mike appeared angry, indignant, and justified about developing a 'friendship' with Linda. He alleged that the relationship was strictly platonic, and the slightly inappropriate texts that Kate read on his phone were just jokes, nothing serious.

Mike felt that Kate was blowing the situation out of proportion. He loved his wife and wanted to move past this insignificant situation. In the same breath that Mike was trying to smooth over his texting situation, he retorted that Kate did not make him feel like a man. He thought that she was ungrateful and inconsiderate given that he helped with chores around the home, cooked dinner, washed Kate's car, and even gave regular back rubs. Mike indicated that when he told other women, including Linda, about what he does for Kate, they seemed to admire and respect him.

One of Mike's specific quarrels with Kate included that she would often mention what she did for the family financially. Kate's rebuttal was that she was not throwing how much money she makes in Mike's face, but that she was stating a fact when situations would come up. Mike *alleged* that it did not matter to him that Kate made more money than he.

In our sessions, Mike had a safe place to explore his true feelings. Eventually, he acknowledged that he hadn't realized it, but he thought that a man's role in the relationship was to be the main provider for his family. His mother did not work outside the home. His father, whom he admired, was the sole financial provider for his family. Mike's anger issues with his wife came from his unawareness of why he was triggered by comments about finances. He didn't realize that the way his childhood functioned impacted the way he thought about his current family.

Regarding Mike's inappropriate conversations, he admitted that he felt that his pride was wounded in his marriage and he needed someone to make him feel 'special.' Mike's issue was really with himself and not his spouse. He learned how to manage his belief systems by increasing his awareness of the thoughts that came to him and acknowledging how his pride contributed to some of his marital problems.

Going forward, Mike increased his communication with Kate about some of the thoughts that went through his head. This increase in communication helped Mike and Kate reconnect. He practiced mindfulness techniques by pausing, breathing, and noticing his thoughts and emotions before he acted. He realized that he was engaging in inappropriate conversations because it made him feel good. He determined that he had engaged in these conversations to get rid of anxious and negative feelings about not being good enough as a man. Mike began to see that entertaining conversations with other women were not helping his marriage. He found it helpful to be mindful of his thoughts and emotions, intentional about doing things that mattered, creative about the way in which he did things that mattered, and self-compassionate every step of the way.

Best Self in Action: Unspoken expectations

IT IS COMMON FOR PEOPLE to carry unspoken expectations about themselves, others, and the world. Notice whether you believe any of the statements below. Notice the prevalence of should statements and their self-righteous and judgmental tone.

- I *should* hold high expectations of the way other people should behave.
- I *should* not have to express my expectations to other people.
- I *should* always prove that I am right.
- I *should* place a high value on being appreciated and recognized for my good works or talents.
- I *should* not have to listen to a different point of view, especially if it doesn't make sense.

If you identified with any of these statements, then you may benefit from being more mindful that the world and other people don't revolve around you. Most things that happen to you and around you have nothing to do with you. Stubborn expectations can set us up to suffer when things do not go our way. Practice living as your Best Self by noticing your expectations of how you think the world, relationships, and other people should behave and holding them lightly.

When it comes to how the world works, consider the quote: 'Expect nothing and accept everything.' This simply means that you will not suffer when you are not attached to an outcome. You are simply discouraged from resisting that which is out of your control. This does not imply that you go through life without any expectations. It is your right to have expectations for how you want to be treated. I encourage you to be mindful of whether your expectations are realistic and intentional about expressing them appropriately at the right place and time.

10

MYOB

MINDING YOUR OWN BUSINESS (MYOB) focuses on protecting your time, finances, and mental and emotional energy. Not only do we have to set and respect our own personal boundaries, but we have to respect others' personal boundaries, too. You will feel much better if you focus on your own affairs. You will have more emotional energy to focus on loving your Self if you are not constantly involved in situations that are not your business. The Williams Brothers gospel group has a song named *Sweep Around* with prophetic lyrics, 'Sweep around your own front door before you sweep around mine.' It is vital to discern when and when not to intervene in someone else's situation.

SHUN RECENTLY SHARED WITH ME a story about her relationship with her mother, Joyce. Shun did not make a lot of money, but what she made, she managed well. Joyce had a history of money mismanagement and continually asked Shun for loans that really were gifts. Joyce was able-bodied and healthy, but had *beer money and champagne taste*. Shun was resentful and angry with her mother for asking her to bail her out of debt repeatedly.

Shun complained that she was not a cheerful giver when it came to her mother. She helped Joyce strictly because she was her mother. Shun knew that she was not protecting her own financial boundaries. She wanted to begin setting limits on her mother and stop bailing her out of every financial crisis. I introduced the four disciplines of Mindful Acceptance to Shun and helped her use them to engage in emotional self-care and intentionally address the situation with her mother. Shun was able to be:

Mindful of her internal sensations when Joyce wanted to borrow money by increasing her awareness of how she felt when Joyce made financial requests. Shun would notice and distance herself from the guilt that bullied her into giving money to her mother even when she knew she was enabling and crippling her.

Intentional about thinking thoughts that support her value system and consider if it is beneficial to her emotional and financial well-being to continue loaning, but really giving, money to her mother.

Self-Compassionate with her emotions and thoughts. She would simply allow herself to feel whatever she felt.

Creative about deciding how she wanted to proceed in her relationship with her mother, such as asserting herself, setting boundaries, and limiting contact.

Helping can be crippling

WE CAN ALL APPRECIATE someone else's willingness to help us. It relieves some pressure and allows us to focus our energy in other areas. How can someone cripple us just by trying to help?

Our independence and growth may be stifled if we are not learning how to accept responsibility for our life situations. I am not suggesting that we refuse needed help and support. However, too much help and support will deprive us of our ability to gain the necessary skills to be successful.

CANDACE WAS A BUSY WOMAN who felt responsible for the lives of her friends and family. She took care of all the household chores. She was the go-to person if her close friends or family members needed a financial loan or any other assistance. Candace's family and friends did not have to want or worry for anything.

Candace appeared to be loved by everyone. Yet, she had a strained relationship with Jim, her only son. How was this possible? Candace had given him everything and done everything for him. If there was an issue with one of his friends, Candace was there. If there was an issue with a sports coach, Candace was there. If Jim had an issue with a teacher, Candace was there.

Candace's involvement in her son's affairs was not healthy. Every time Candace tried to help her son, the situation would become about her and she would manage it as if it directly impacted her. All Jim had to do was tell her about a problem and she would independently solve it, leaving herself drained and her son emotionally underdeveloped. He was rarely allowed to handle his age-appropriate responsibilities.

As an adult, Jim behaved with entitlement and ungratefulness. He blamed his mother for his poor life decisions. As a married adult, Jim had marital difficulties. A contributor to their marriage difficulty was that his wife didn't appreciate his mother's personal boundary violations. Candace continued to bail Jim out of financial situations because he was living beyond his means. His wife wanted Candace to allow him to figure out his own financial solution rather than running to his rescue. Jim's wife was aware that her husband would not learn how to manage his finances as long as his mother continued to rescue him.

Candace needed to identify why she would not allow other people to handle their own business. Did she have a difficult time tolerating emotional tension in other people? Was she afraid of being seen as unkind for not offering to help? Does Candace need to distance herself from the thoughts that caused her to become consumed with her son's affairs?

Candace thought that she was being helpful. She was unaware of the negative effects of her helpfulness. Being too helpful can have a crippling effect on other people. She needed to determine what was her business, when to intervene in someone's life, and when she needed to mind her own business!

Candace was obviously too involved in her son's life and violating his personal boundaries. She had violated her son's right for autonomy, which in turn hindered his growth. Over time, both Candace and her son began to feel empty inside. Their emotional energy and resources were drained.

Candace explored her values and discovered what was most important. She became mindful of her value to help people. We talked about how her value, if overused, could hurt instead of help other people. Candace considered the possible negative outcomes of helping too much the next time a situation with her son presented itself. She asked herself, 'Based upon my experiences with my son, would my help be assistance or hindrance?' This statement allowed Candace to practice using flexibility in her behaviors.

Candace learned the four disciplines of Mindful Acceptance and developed the skills she needed to tolerate the uncomfortable feeling that she experienced when loved ones appeared to be in crisis situations. She was aware that her mind might tell her that other people would not love her if she didn't save them from their own issues. She memorized self-compassionate coping statements to help her sit with the anxiety about her current and past behavior. Candace was intentional about balancing her value of helping with that of personal autonomy and responsibility. Candace proudly boasts a healthy relationship with herself and with her son. Once she began spending less time trying to solve other people's problems and more time handling her own business, she had more time and energy to focus on taking care of herself.

The empowerment of genuine support

THERE IS A SIGNIFICANT DIFFERENCE between support and meddling. Support includes listening empathetically and non-judgmentally. Support is patiently listening to concerns and not immediately providing advice. Support is not always jumping in and trying to fix the situation. Support allows a person the opportunity to figure out how to manage her own situation. Support is uplifting and motivating. Support is trusting in the other person's ability to make good decisions. Genuine support validates the other person's experience and identifies with his situation.

Meddling is listening with judgments. Meddling is not hearing the other person's concerns but considering ways to solve the problem while the other person is still talking about the problem. Meddling does not provide emotional support. Meddling takes over the situation as if it were your own. Meddling has more to do with satisfying your own need for stability, order, and control than helping the other person.

Support feels good to both parties. Meddling may leave the meddler feeling negative inside if the person in need doesn't behave the way she feels that she *should*. Inadvertently, the receiver of meddling may feel incompetent and inept. A history of experiences that send the message of incompetence may lead a person to believe that he is incompetent.

I have found that people who are prone to meddling can be quite judgmental. They often think they know how things *should* be done and they can do a better job at fixing the problem than anyone else. Meddlers will often think, but not say out loud: 'James is incompetent. He doesn't know how to obtain a home loan without my help.' Most people interfere in other people's lives under the guise of wanting to help. It is not obvious to most people, but this meddler's desire to help, take over, or manage someone else's business is often more about the meddler than the other person. The meddler experiences fear and anxiety about the other person's failure as if it were her own. The meddler doesn't know where she ends and the other person begins, which is a huge personal boundary issue.

There are times when it is helpful to pour energy, time, and finances into others, especially when you have taken care of your own emotional needs. It becomes tricky when you are simply *saying* that you are emotionally full, but your overall sense of happiness reveals something different. You may be fooling others about what you really have to give, but you can't fool your Self. You are not prioritizing your emotional self-care if you are not making time to engage in behaviors that you know are constructive, such as exercise and proper nutrition. It is not about what you are *saying* to others. It is about actively and consciously looking within, assessing how you have been treating your mind, body, and soul, and becoming aware of whether what you are giving to others is truly extra.

Refusing to take personal responsibility for parts of someone's life or not bailing them out financially are some of the most challenging intentional behaviors to practice. Many of my clients have presented several internal barriers to why they struggle with allowing people to manage their own lives. One protest is that their family members will feel unloved. The second protest that I hear is concern for negative outcomes in the lives of family members. Both protests are valid.

Because the meddler's mind thinks she is helping the other person, it will tell the meddler the sneakiest and most manipulative things to encourage her to meddle:

- What type of person would I be if I refused to help?
- Wouldn't I want someone to help me if the shoe were on the other foot?
- What if I could prevent the other person from harming herself?

IT IS HELPFUL TO INCREASE YOUR AWARENESS of how you feel about the person that you want to help. Do you know that you love him? Have you shown love to him? Do you feel that you need to continue to prove your love to this other person by caretaking and helping? By increasing mindfulness, you will be able to distance your Self from what your mind is telling you, look at your experience, affirm the present moment, and make better decisions.

We are each responsible for our own adult lives. We are talking about adults here, not children. You do not have control over what happens to the other person's life, and you cannot predict the future. Who is to say that rescuing a person from her own story will prevent something bad from happening to her? Rescuing prevents a person from learning to take personal responsibility for her actions. It sends the message that the person being helped is incapable.

LESLIE WAS A SUCCESSFUL SOCIAL WORKER. Her father's blood sugar was often high and out of control. Leslie purchased her father a gym membership so that he could gain control of his diabetes. He refused to go to the gym. Leslie was frustrated when she discovered that her father was refusing to do his part to contribute to his physical well-being. She worried that her father may die from diabetic complications. This fear of her father dying made her angrier. Thus, she entertained other ways to *make* him see that he was slowly killing himself. If you catch yourself trying to *make* an adult do something, then you are heading toward a personal boundary violation, even if it is for the other person's own good.

Leslie and her father began to argue often, making it difficult for them to be around each other. Her father didn't appear to see his situation in the same bleak manner. Leslie's anger and anxiety become so overwhelming that she decided to schedule an appointment with me. I provided compassion and validation to Leslie for the hurt that she was experiencing from her relationship with her father. I encouraged her to employ self-compassion for the boundary violations and the pain of their current relationship. Leslie explored whether she had been designated as the primary caretaker for her father. Leslie agreed that she didn't have the right to take over her father's life. After learning the disciplines of Mindful Acceptance, she concluded that her father's life was just that, *his life*. Further, Leslie experimented with ways to practice patience and cope with difficult emotions.

The difficult emotion for Leslie was the fear of what would happen to her father if he did not properly manage his diabetes. Leslie learned how to notice her thoughts and emotions without becoming over- whelmed and sucked into believing every scary thought that came to her mind and uncomfortable sensation that flowed through her body. The intentional practice of patience and emotional distancing allowed Leslie to calm down when she felt like acting on her emotions of fear and anxiety and instead engage in self-care behaviors.

Best Self in Practice: Do you help too much?

THERE IS A FINE LINE BETWEEN helping and meddling. Use the questions below to help you notice whether you are helping or meddling. Be mindful if you experience intense frustration when friends that you have helped don't behave the way you think they *should* behave. This may signal that you have been meddling with strings attached and not helping unconditionally.

- Would you be frustrated if your college-aged child doesn't show gratitude and appreciation for your financial support?
- If you have helped your significant other look for a job, would it upset you if they did not take the job search seriously?
- If you have helped your mother pay for her cell phone bill, would you become angry every time she went to the casino?
- Do you cover for your partner if s/he gets drunk, feeling bad about lying to family and friends?

If you answered yes to any of these questions, then be mindful of your helping behaviors and why you feel compelled to help. If you and the helped party are not experiencing any crippling effects or difficulties, then maybe this situation works for you.

LET'S PRACTICE MINDING OUR OWN BUSINESS and leaving others alone, unless it is mutually beneficial in both the short-term and long-term. You will know if you are meddling if you expect the person that you helped to behave a certain way.

Be mindful of when helping behaviors become extreme, which is more serious than just helping too much. In Melody Beattie's book, *Codependent No More: How to Stop Controlling Others and Start Caring for Yourself,* she describes extreme helpfulness as co-dependency and lists several characteristics of codependent traits which include, but are not limited to: care-taking, low self-worth, denial, poor boundaries, and controlling. Codependent traits are most noticeable in relationships where one partner is addicted to substances such as drugs and alcohol, or activities such as gambling, video games, or sex. Codependency may exist more subtly in parent-child, platonic, and romantic relationships without addictions.

11

RESPONDING TO OTHERS

MINDFUL ACCEPTANCE ALLOWS US to dislike a person's behavior while doing what we need to do to take care of ourselves. Mindful Acceptance prevents suffering because we no longer depend on the actions of others for our emotional well-being.

In the past, I had clients explore difficult relationships with one of their parents. I, and many other clinicians, describe this process as *family of origin exploration*. For example, June had a very strained relationship with her mother, Gail. June was the second middle daughter of five children. When I met her, she was married with one child. She described her mother as manipulative, selfish, self-centered, and attention-seeking. June acknowledged that as a child, she did not have any other choice but to deal with her mother.

As an adult, June chose to maintain minimum contact with Gail. She had mixed feelings because sometimes she wanted a close, healthy relationship with her. June's desire was heightened when she saw other loving mother-adult daughter relationships. June's mind told her that she *should* have a close relationship with her mother and that she *should* be a better daughter. She tried for years to obey her mind and develop a close relationship with her mother, mainly out of guilt. As June attempted to repair the relationship, Gail kept overstepping boundaries by frequently providing unsolicited advice and refusing to call before coming over to visit.

When I first met June, she divulged that she was in a place where she would be ok if she never saw her mother again. Cutting ties with a close family member, friend, or romantic partner can be a difficult decision. For some people, it demonstrates emotional self-care. This intimately personal decision must consider the nature of the relationship and whether you had established effective boundaries in the past. Mindful Acceptance increases our awareness of our own behavior, and we become intentional about what we currently need or do not need. June's situation was not severe enough for her to justify ending the relationship completely. However, the dysfunction of the relationship was affecting June's emotional well-being.

June couldn't genuinely talk to anyone about how she felt about Gail and their relationship because she thought that people would judge her and tell her how she *should* respond to her mother. She worried that her Christian friends would remind her of the Bible verse, 'Honor thy mother and father or thy days shall be numbered.' June said that it infuriated her when people used the Bible to make her feel worse than she already felt about her relationship with her mother.

I offered June a safe, non-judgmental, and neutral environment to explore her feelings about her mother, the nature of their relationship, and the way her mind had been bossing her around. Over time, she experienced genuine peace about her feelings toward Gail and their relationship. June recalled that increasing her awareness of her true feelings and safely exploring them allowed her to dislike Gail less. Soon, she was comfortable with her position and was not moved by other people's opinions of her situation. June could finally be content with a mother-daughter relationship that was perfectly imperfect.

Mindful Acceptance does not mean tolerating someone's bad behavior. The only thing that you have to deal with is your own emotions and thoughts. If someone's poor behavior is having a negative impact on you, remove yourself from harm's way! I do not expect or want you to accept mistreatment because 'That's just the way she is' or 'It is what it is.'

After you have become aware of someone's behavior, you have the power to be intentional and creative about making an informed decision about how to best address the situation.

Tough decisions

WHAT DO YOU DO IF YOU ARE EXPERIENCING toxic behavior from an adult child? This is always a tough question, especially when addiction and mental illness are involved. Each situation is unique, and there is not a one-size-fits-all response for this type of situation.

KYLA VISITED ME AFTER several intense events had occurred with her 29-year-old son, Tim, who was diagnosed with bipolar disorder. Tim was not consistently following up with his medication and therapy. He continued to engage in disrespectful behaviors toward his mother. Kyla would often open up her home to Tim after he would have an argument with his housemates. Kyla would allow Tim to return under certain conditions, which included following the rules of her house. Tim repeatedly defied the rules of her house by having company present when his mother was not home, coming to the house after curfew, and smoking cigarettes in the home. Kyla continued to set boundaries and limits with Tim until she became fed up.

The final straw was when Tim had a party at her home while Kyla was out of town. Alcohol and drugs were involved, and the police called Kyla while she was on vacation. After this episode, Kyla informed Tim that he had to find a place of his own and could not bounce back and forth between her home and his friend's home.

Kyla was torn. She struggled with being hooked by thoughts telling her that she was a failure as a mother. She tormented herself, trying to figure out where she went wrong as a parent. By the time Kyla visited me, she was at her wit's end. She was angry with herself and her son. Kyla and I worked a great deal on self-compassion so that she could begin to extend compassion to Tim. We explored what about Tim's behavior and their relationship was triggering something inside her. Kyla worked on being mindful of her unconscious and automatic responses to Tim. She became intentional about how she dealt with her son. She no longer engaged in shouting matches. Kyla began to calmly express herself and refuse to engage in back and forth rebuttals. This restraint and intentional, value-directed behavior provided Kyla with inner peace, and it modeled assertive communication to Tim.

Although Kyla informed Tim that they needed a break from living together, she was able to tell him that she would always love him and support him in the best way that she could. Kyla made it clear to Tim that her support might not look the way that he wanted it to look, but she would always love him and have his best interest at heart. Kyla was able to express her value of encouraging healthy independence and separation from Tim in the service of him learning how to become a self-sufficient and mature adult.

Worrying about someone else's problem is not going to help him or you move in a meaningful direction.

WE HAVE TO BE REAL WITH OURSELVES to know if we are able to deal with the consequences of tough decisions such as letting go of a loved one. We can learn to approve and accept ourselves so that it doesn't matter what other people think of us.

It's a beautiful feeling to *want* other people in our lives, but not *need* them. If we think that our survival depends on other people being in our lives, we will go to all costs to survive, even if it means ignoring our own emotional self-care and worth. If we know that we will be happy with or without another person, we are more willing to engage in rational and intentional behavior that doesn't minimize or ignore our emotional health. We don't have to fear being alone because if we are open to connection and meeting people, we will meet someone who accepts us as much as we accept ourselves.

Letting go doesn't have to be physical. It could be a mental 'letting go' of trying to control someone or her situation. We can learn to be willing to allow things to happen that are out of our control and sit with our present reality. Worrying about someone else's problem is not going to help him or you move in a meaningful direction. Worrying gives the illusion that you are helping. You are making it worse by wasting time reviewing scenarios that may or may not happen instead of doing something that could lead to meaningful change.

Forgiveness is liberating

MINDFUL ACCEPTANCE INVITES US to let go of anger and resentment, which frees up mental and emotional space to love and be loved. Forgiveness is the mental letting go of psychological bondage to another person and no longer waiting for, or caring whether someone makes amends, apologizes, or repays you. Forgiveness is letting go of the attempt to recreate a different, better past.

Forgiveness means that you have released the person who has offended or harmed you so he no longer owes you anything. This person will no longer have the power to control your emotions or behaviors. This does not mean that it would be wise to be friends with this person or that you have forgotten what he did. Forgiveness simply means that this person is no longer occupying space in your mind, rent-free.

'Holding onto anger is like drinking poison
and expecting the other person to die.'
— Anonymous proverb

FORGIVENESS LIBERATES YOU from the other person to live your life fully and without negative attachments to her. This other person has possibly gone on with her life and doesn't know you have given her power to control your emotions and maintain free occupancy in your mind. When we are holding on to an issue with someone, hurt is dormant, but anger is usually what maintains the chains of bondage. Free yourself and free the other person, and you will live a more peaceful and rewarding life.

PETER, A 50-YEAR-OLD MARRIED MAN with two children, came to visit me about his anger issues. He had never spoken with a therapist, but his friends and family strongly encouraged him to speak with someone. Peter had issues with holding grudges. Events that had occurred more than ten years ago were still fresh in his mind, and he often thought that people were out to get him.

After talking with Peter, I became aware that his insecurities were maintaining his anger. He was the oldest of three siblings who were financially successful, while Peter was living paycheck to paycheck. Much of Peter's anger at the world stemmed from him blaming other people for his situation. Peter's mind was doing one of the things it has evolved to do: assign blame. I helped Peter become aware that his mind was not defective or behaving abnormally. Peter learned the discipline of self-compassion and forgave himself of unhealthy past decisions. He became mindful that his misdirected anger was really at himself, not other people. Additionally, Peter realized that once he let go of the anger that he had with himself that he would be a kinder and nicer person to those around him.

Mindful Acceptance is a personal process whereby we release resentment towards ourselves, others, and the world because of how things *should* be. Things are the way they are; good or bad, it is what it is. Let's change what we can and mindfully accept what we cannot. Who are we to say how things *should* be? In the same breath, if you don't like the way something is, and you have the ability to change it, then change it.

Letting go of *should* thinking

TARA AND ANNA CAME TO VISIT ME because of depressive symptoms and a strained relationship. When they first met, Anna had informed Tara that she was no longer interested in dating men. After about nine months, Tara discovered that Anna had cheated on her with one of her former male partners. Tara was hurt on several levels. She felt betrayed. Worse, Anna kept telling Tara that she *should* have known that she couldn't completely give up sex with men. Furthermore, Anna claimed that she wasn't in a relationship with the male partner; it was only sex.

It was unrealistic for Anna to think that Tara *should* have known that she would be unfaithful in their relationship. I helped Anna realize that she had been using *should* thinking as an excuse to be unfaithful. Anna and Tara became mindful of their personal experiences, intentional about noticing what their mind was telling them, compassionate towards themselves and others, and creative in their behaviors. Fortunately, Anna and Tara were willing to make the relationship work. They created a relationship vision based on their values and recommitted to being faithful and engaging in loving and kind behaviors.

Always know that you have choices and you are responsible for taking care of your emotional and physical needs. Be creative and learn to think outside the box. Move away from a stuck mindset to an options mindset. Begin to believe that *a way can be made out of no way,* which is an old Southern Baptist saying meaning that God will always provide regardless of the circumstance. Look over your life and try to remember when a door had been opened for you when you could not see how it would be opened. Be mindful of these situations.

If you need support, it is up to you to reach out for it. Don't expect people to ask what you need. They may, and it is nice when they do, but please do not wait around on someone to take care of your needs.

How to win the blame game

WE GET CAUGHT UP in the mind game of blaming someone else for our reality. If she would just 'stop doing this' or 'start doing that,' then I would be happy! This behavior has negative effects on our emotional and mental health. We are like a cat chasing its tail around in circles. At least the cat appears to enjoy chasing its tail. Most of us do not like being caught up in the game of trying to force another adult to behave the way we think and feel they *should* behave. *The only way to win the blame game is to choose not to play.*

As much as we want to believe that we have control over another person's behavior, at the end of the day, he will do as he chooses. We have to adjust to the fact that we are unable to change other people as a way to change our reality.

Recently, I was driving to pick up one of my daughters and my mind began to wonder. I did not ask for these thoughts to come to my mind, but they came anyway. My mind began to think of how I wanted to spend more time working in the office, but instead, I was driving my daughters around from one activity to the next. I became frustrated and began to blame my husband for my sullen mood. I was thinking that my partner gets to stay at work as long as he likes while I have to alter my work schedule around the children's schedule. Yes, I was going down that rabbit hole. I had to catch myself before I became too entangled with my thoughts. Because I began to feel frustrated, I asked myself, 'What would make me happy at this moment?' My responses were first about what my partner could do differently. I then remembered to be mindful that I cannot change other people, only myself!

I decided to ask myself a different question. What could I do for myself in that moment to help me deal with feeling overworked and overwhelmed? I intentionally regained contact with the present moment where I noticed that I had everything I needed. Then, I decided to commit to scheduling time-out breaks that allowed me to relax and do something nice for myself. The thought of my time-out breaks brought me joy. I reminded myself of the futile attempt of chasing happiness. It was ok for me to feel frustrated when I thought about all my responsibilities. It would not have been ok for me to remain stuck in frustration and then take it out on my spouse or children. It was not ok for me to blame my moment of frustration and unhappiness on my spouse.

---

*Blaming other people for our emotions
will not get us far in life.*

BLAME DISEMPOWERS US. It is empowering to think, 'I can do anything that I practice and put my mind to doing,' rather than, 'If someone would just give me my big break, I will be happy and successful.'

Regarding interpersonal conflict, it is helpful to focus on how you could do things differently to influence the outcome of a situation rather than focusing on what someone else *could* or *should* do. It is healthier to consider what you can do differently if you want a different outcome. Sometimes, the situation just calls for us to self-soothe, which means to calm ourselves down before making major decisions or confronting other people.

Think about the last time that you were angry with someone. If you are able to take yourself back to that situation, do you remember where your attention was focused? Were you focused on what the other person did? If so, that is normal and habitual for most of us. It takes intentional and courageous behavior to channel your attention towards what it is about you that made you susceptible to being offended by what the other person did. Another introspective question to ask yourself is, 'What mental knots have been triggered in this interaction with the other person?' This type of introspection will help you transform pain into purpose, untie mental knots, and remove hot buttons and triggers. Introspection is not about blaming yourself or anyone else. It is the intentional and compassionate behavior of looking within in order to heal, transform, and grow.

THERESA'S SITUATION HIT HOME WITH ME. She was a 35-year-old working mother of three young children, ages 7, 5, and 3. She had devoted her life to managing her family and raising her children. She dropped them off and picked them up from school. She handled planning the meals, cooking, and cleaning the house. Theresa took the children to all their extracurricular activities, which she had to take off early from work to do. Theresa was frustrated with her partner because she felt that her partner didn't contribute as much to the maintenance of the children as she did. Theresa grumbled to her friends about her situation. She resented not having enough time for herself.

First, Theresa was correct. Her life was not fair. We can move on when we accept the unfairness of life, and refuse to waste energy focusing on it. There is no need in brooding over a fact. Brooding just breeds resentment and frustration.

Over the years, I have worked with families of all shapes and sizes, and the many tasks of parenting are never evenly divided. Theresa needed to focus less on her partner and more on changing herself. Yes, it would be nice if her partner assisted with the children and household and made time for her to have by herself. I did advocate that Theresa ask for what she needed from her partner. I suggested that Theresa actively do what she needed to do for herself to feel better and experience lasting happiness. Best Self activities could include journaling, practicing yoga, reading, knitting, painting, refusing over-commitment, or reconnecting with friends.

Behaving as your Best Self will look different for different people. If you are trying to figure out your emotional self-care needs, ask yourself, what do you not do anymore that you used to enjoy before you were partnered or had children.

Theresa was encouraged to increase personal responsibility for her happiness and consider where could she lighten her load. She initially protested that she couldn't scale back on any behaviors because it all had to be done. Everything *doesn't* have to be done right now. Theresa needed to, as Stephen Covey says, *Put First Things First,* and make time for herself by any means necessary. If this meant that the family had to order out dinner one night instead of her cooking, then so be it! Everyone will survive! Theresa realized that she would be a better wife and parent if she spent more time engaged in emotional self-care. If you are like Theresa, try out emotional self-care and see how you can become a better parent and partner.

The Serenity Prayer

I AM FAMILIAR WITH THE SERENITY PRAYER because I was raised in a household with a father who was addicted to whatever drug was available. I've changed the first line from 'God grant me,' to 'God of my understanding grant me,' so that people can customize the prayer to their own faith. 'God of my understanding' can be applied to any belief in a power higher than oneself.

> *God of my understanding, grant me the serenity to*
> *Accept the things that I cannot change; the*
> *Courage to change the things that I can;*
> *and the wisdom to know the difference.*

We are sometimes unaware of what we cannot change and need to be more mindful. We get caught up in trying to manage other people's lives and feel angry about past events that cannot be undone so much so that we can lose sight of ourselves. Let's unpack the Serenity Prayer:

> *God of my understanding, grant me the serenity to*
> *Accept the things that I cannot change*

We do not have control over another person's behavior, thoughts, or emotions. We do not have control over our intrusive thoughts and emotions. We do not have control over what has happened in the past or what will happen in the future.

> *Courage to change the things that I can*

We can change the amount of time we choose to spend with people who are negative, including family members. We can change our own actions. We can change our perspectives. We can change the amount of energy that we give to intrusive thoughts.

We can change whom we allow into our inner circle of friends. We can change what we allow into our spirit. We can be intentional about feeding our spirit with positive interactions and positive thoughts. We can change and control our own happiness.

and the wisdom to know the difference.

Wisdom invites us to be kind to others without being unkind to ourselves. Wisdom guides us to help others without crippling their independence and self-sufficiency. Wisdom is what inspires us to follow our values. Wisdom is not found in knowledge, but in experience.

Best Self in Action: Doing what works

ARE YOU ABLE TO ACCEPT OTHERS just the way they are today? Bella has been in a committed relationship for a little over two years, and her partner is no longer as considerate as he was early in the relationship. He no longer gives regular back rubs or brings home small trinkets of love to let her know that he thought about her during the day. What does Bella do?

- Does she hold on to how things used to be?
- Does she acknowledge her current situation and be intentional about dealing with it accordingly, which may be to communicate her needs and see what happens?
- Does she nag her partner about changing?

- Does she accept things the way they are because 'it is what it is?
- Does she leave the relationship?

There is no right or wrong answer, *per se*. There is a 'what works best for Bella and what doesn't work for Bella' response. Mindful Acceptance is about knowing when to physically or mentally 'let go' of people, places, and things that are not working for you. It is about creatively figuring out how to best meet your needs and what does work for you. Every day, practice noticing your habitual behaviors and asking yourself, 'Is this behavior working for me?' If the answer is no, consider doing something that does work for you.

The Four Disciplines in Romance

MINDFUL ACCEPTANCE STRENGTHENS our relationships by increasing our awareness of our values and discovering what we truly want and need from a partner. I have found that a thoughtful exploration of Dr. Gary Chapman's *Five Love Languages* is quite helpful in getting clients to think of what they need in a romantic relationship. Chapman's ideas are not complex, and most people find the process of discovery to be constructive and uplifting. The five love languages are words of affirmation, acts of service, receiving gifts, quality time, and physical touch.

People communicate love in a specific language: saying and hearing affirming words, doing things for their partner, giving and receiving little (or big) things, spending time together, and snuggling. A curious thing about humans that you may not know: many couples don't naturally speak the same love language. Someone who gives and receives love through speaking kind words may not appreciate or know that her partner would rather receive or give a little gift. It makes sense that simply knowing the languages of love can help couples communicate better. Learning to speak your partner's love languages can take your relationship to another level of happiness.

I've had clients categorize their relationship values within Dr. Gary Chapman's five love languages to help them determine what's most important to them. I've often disclosed to my clients that, for me, loyalty and being made a priority, which fall under Chapman's acts of service and quality time love languages, are non-negotiable for me. As much as I complain about my husband not cleaning around the house, that is not a deal breaker for me. I have to remember to be mindful of all the wonderful ways that my husband communicates his love for me when I find myself being frustrated by something that doesn't really matter in the big scheme of things. I increase my intentional thoughts to help me cope with my emotions and behave lovingly, even when my mind tells me to emotionally punish him for frustrating me.

MARSHALL LOVES GIVING GIFTS TO HIS WIFE, Lily, for special occasions such as Valentine's Day and Christmas, but gifts is not her primary love language. He may not ever tell her how much he loves receiving gifts, and simply expect her to show her love by giving him thoughtful gifts during the holidays. If it's a typical marriage, Lily may appreciate the gifts, but she really glows when Marshall takes a long walk with her and gives her his full attention. Lily's love language is quality time.

Both Marshall and Lily are communicating love, but are like two ships passing in the night. Their lack of communication can cause real problems, because Marshall will be showing his love for his wife by giving gifts and expecting gifts in return while Lily expects lots of quality time.

Marshall's mind may try to get him to believe that Lily doesn't really love him because she doesn't shower him with gifts or respond the way that he expects to his thoughtfulness. If your partner doesn't speak your primary love language, you will want to communicate your needs. If you communicate your needs, and your partner is still unable or unwilling to meet them, then you may want to reevaluate your relationship or figure out other creative ways to get your needs met (that doesn't jeopardize the relationship or your values). If you like to be affirmed often, and your partner isn't very verbal, it might be helpful to have people in your platonic friend or family circle who are affirmative.

Knowing your role in relationships

DO YOU KNOW YOUR ROLE in your current relationship? Engaging in emotional self-care means that you are mindful and intentional about knowing your role in your relationship. Are you the breadwinner? Do you take the lead on housekeeping? Are you the first to apologize and extend the olive branch after arguments? Are you the feisty one? Your awareness of your role does not mean that you like it. At least if you are aware of it, then you are in a position to change it, if you so choose, by being self-compassionate and creative about choosing intentional thoughts that will lead to wise, intentional behaviors. You do not have to be glued to any rigid roles. Continue to ask yourself, 'Is this role working for me?' This awareness will prevent you from being stuck and losing yourself in any particular role.

Many people will think that this *should not* be an issue; however, it comes up quite often in my office and in many social settings. What if you are a female in a heterosexual relationship, and you make more money than your partner? Growing up, you might have witnessed your father financially providing for your family, so this scenario became your expectation.

The Four Disciplines of Romance

DAPHNE INITIALLY THOUGHT IT WOULD BE SHALLOW to focus on who made more money in her relationship, but over time, she noticed that it bothered her. She began behaving disrespectfully towards Joshua because her mind told her that he was not successful. Daphne became condescending in her dialogue with him. Her mind told her that Joshua was child-like because he was unable to behave in the way she thought that he *should* behave. Many people have discovered just how toxic a relationship can become when one partner is critical towards the other. John Gottman, in *The Seven Principles for Making Marriage Work*, lists criticism as one of the four predictors of divorce.

The best place to begin is with your Self.

YOUR MIND MAY TELL YOU that you *should* be with someone who can provide abundantly for you. Your chatterbox might try to make you afraid that if you lost your job, you would not have financial support from your partner. This probably is not even half of what your mind might tell you, but I think you get the gist.

One way of dealing with this type of situation is to get out of your head and look at your experience. It might be helpful to ask yourself if your partner demonstrates financial responsibility. Notice whether your partner has been financially helpful in your relationship although he doesn't make the most money. Another suggestion is to notice all the thoughts that your mind is telling you about your partner's financial situation, and ask yourself if it is helpful to believe, dwell upon, or get caught up in those thoughts. If the answer is yes, then continue doing what works. If the answer is no, then begin to notice your thoughts as words, images, and symbols, and be intentional about holding those thoughts lightly as you would hold a prickly cactus.

If you do not like your current role in the relationship, first make sure that you are aware of your values, wants, and needs, *and then clearly communicate what you need from your partner.* A heart to heart discussion about your relationship values can save a relationship, or help end it at the right time. Remember, as much as your partner cares about you, she will not be able to read your mind. Be mindful, intentional, self-compassionate, and creative in communicating your personal, emotional, and physical needs in the relationship.

The best place to begin is with your Self. Once you have taken care of how you respond to a situation, you can move on to addressing your partner's role. This means asking yourself just how serious is this situation and why is it so serious to you. Is it worth the internal angst that you are experiencing? What can you change about your perception to make this situation no longer a problem for you, given that safety and disrespect are not an issue? How can this situation be made better that has nothing to do with the other person changing? Specially, what can you creatively do for yourself within your chosen value system to be at peace with the current situation?

BEFORE HAVING CHILDREN, I used to do all the laundry. It wasn't a huge deal. After children, it became too much to do laundry for the entire family. My husband has a habit of leaving his clothes wherever he takes them off rather than putting them directly in the hamper. I have been creative in trying to help him in getting his clothes to a hamper. I have purchased sorting hampers for his closet, and we have a laundry hamper in our bedroom. We have a laundry chute in the bathroom that goes directly down to the laundry room. Nevertheless, my husband's clothes still end up in random piles. I have made it clear that I refuse to hunt down his clothes when it is time to do laundry. If he wants his clothes washed, guess what? He will need to put them in one of the many, strategically placed laundry hampers. Over time, I stopped nagging about the random dirty pile of clothes and started doing what I needed to do for myself, such as setting limits about what I would do, making laundry hampers accessible, and changing my focus. He eventually realized that if he wanted clean clothes, then they would need to make it to a laundry hamper.

The 80/20 concept in relationships

I LOVE THINKING ABOUT THE 80/20 CONCEPT when it comes to relationships. I had heard of it before, but Tyler Perry's movie, *Why Did I Get Married*, allowed me to see it, quite exaggerated and dramatically, in action. This 80/20 rule originated with Vilfredo Pareto, an Italian economist and engineer. He applied this rule to wealth distribution, noting that 20% of the population in Italy owned 80% of the land. Later, management theorists have applied the rule to workflow, arguing that 80% of effects come from 20% of causes. This rule has helped managers narrow their focus to increase productivity. However, the rule is sometimes colloquially used to apply to relationships.

Familiarizing yourself with the 80/20 concept in relationships may be a game changer. This concept suggests that, in a *healthy* relationship, you get a whopping 80% of what you need from the other person while the other 20% of your needs will not be met by the other person. Healthy is the operative word here. I am not talking about a relationship where emotional or physical abuse, addiction, recurrent infidelity, or untreated mental illness are involved. Note that the 80/20 percentage is arbitrary. It could be 70/30, 80/20, or 90/10. The gist is that, if we are in a relatively healthy relationship, the other person will not meet 100% of our needs, but the other person could meet the majority of our needs. The unmet percentage is where you would take an active role in taking care of your emotional needs. For sake of familiarity, we will just stick with 80/20.

The grass is not always greener on the other side.

AS HUMANS, WE DESIRE what we don't have, often to our detriment, by overlooking what we do have. Relationships and people are not perfect! Which is in your 80% of importance: stability or excitement?

To the individual who wants a 'lady in the street and a freak between the sheets': if she is that freaky, I'm not sure how much of a lady in the street she is, and you probably aren't the only one she is freaking. Which is your 80% of importance: being a lady or being freaky?

To the individual who wants a chivalrous, rich guy with 'swagger' and panache: I'm not sure if he will be rich, he may be 'fake rich,' but I don't know about '*rich* rich.' Mr. Swagger may not be only swagging for you, but swagging for others.

Which is your 80% of importance: being rich and chivalrous or having swagger?

As we mature, we begin to notice that we cannot have our cake and ice cream from the same person. Healthy individuals in healthy relationships realize the importance of having a strong social support system outside one's mate because our mate cannot be our 'everything.'

Discovering the flip side

LET'S EXPLORE SOME PERSONALITY TRAITS and their flip sides, beginning with a brief background on trait theory. According to trait theory, traits are defined as habitual patterns of behaviors, thoughts, and emotions that are stable over time.

Trait theorists can be traced back as far as Hippocrates; however, Gordon Allport is considered to be one of the first modern trait theorists. He came up with a list of 4,000 traits, which was considered overwhelming for researchers to measure. Other researchers followed Allport, such as Raymond Cattell whose 16 personality factors was too complicated for many researchers, and Hans Eysenck's three-factor theory, which researchers said was too restricted in range. The five-factor theory or the Big Five theory was eventually developed to describe individual personality traits that can be measured along a continuum. The Big Five personality traits are extraversion, agreeableness, conscientiousness, neuroticism, and openness to experience. A common relationship challenge occurs when partners have dominant traits that are at opposite ends of the continuum, such as extraversion and introversion.

It is a beautiful thing to appreciate the differences that each partner brings to the table.

IF YOU ARE UNABLE TO APPRECIATE your differences, you might find yourself focusing on differences that your mind might want you to perceive as negatives. Notice your own thoughts about your partner and your relationship. If you notice that your mind is telling you unhealthy stories about your partner or your relationship, then you may want to consider different self-help approaches.

The traditional *cognitive behavior* approach asks you to determine if there is any distortion or error in your thoughts. Is there any truth or evidence to the thought, and is this a thought that you believe 100%? The aim of this process is to help you identify, challenge, and replace thoughts that are not working for you. One possible drawback to this approach is that you might find your Self caught up in an internal struggle with your thoughts. Some people become frustrated when they realize that they cannot technically replace their thoughts and prevent them from ever returning.

Many thoughts are automatic and out of our control. They come and go as they choose. If you are exerting energy battling with your thoughts, how are you engaging in behavior that is meaningful and important? If this approach helps you reclaim your Best Self, then by all means, continue. If this does not work for you, I encourage you to take a step further and consider moving beyond the current content of your thoughts and consider changing your relationship with them.

The *acceptance and commitment* approach to this situation offers a different solution to deal with troublesome thoughts. Consider changing your relationship with the problematic thoughts by noticing that you are not your thoughts. You are much more than just your thoughts. Once you become aware that your thoughts are not your enemy or your friend, then you can simply notice and name them. That is, you can simply recognize the thought that someone is a selfish without over-identifying with it. You can then experience some distance from the words and images that are your thoughts in order to make healthy decisions for your Self and your relationship.

Mundane challenges in healthy relationships often highlight something in us that we really need to address.

WHAT IF A WIFE MAKES AN INNOCENT suggestion to her husband concerning how he manages his money? If he becomes defensive and responds, 'I don't need help managing my money. I've been handling my finances way before you came along.' What do you think this snippy response was about? Was it really about the suggestion? Was he raised in the household with a controlling caregiver? Was his household dysfunctional because of addiction, mental illness, an ill relative, or abuse? Increasing awareness of our own sensitivities and being intentional and self-compassionate will help stabilize our relationships. Notice the thoughts that are coming to your mind and what your mind is telling you in these situations. Just notice. Then, commit to engaging in and to receiving kind and loving behaviors.

If you have a conflict in your relationship, it will be helpful to increase your awareness of what it is about your past experiences that you might be bringing to the problem. Ask yourself, 'Where does this problem lie in my past? Is it within me or outside me?' It is more empowering if the conflict is within yourself because you will have the ability to make changes. If the problem is outside yourself, you will have less power to change the situation.

It is unrealistic, unfair, and insensitive to expect our partner or other people to be aware of our every little nuance and peccadillo. Suppose, as a child, you never felt that you were as good as your older sibling. You felt that you had to work twice as hard and still didn't measure up. As an adult, you might feel attacked if someone questions your decision about something. The question could have been perceived as innocent to someone else, but to you, it was a personal attack. In this type of situation, it might be helpful to step back and reassess why the question bothered you the way it did. The less time you spend focusing on why someone said something and the more time you spend seeking why the statement bothered you, the quicker you will be able to enjoy being your Best Self.

People will not want to be around you if they feel that they must walk on eggshells in your presence. Practice increasing awareness of your sensitivities and taking steps towards minimizing and eliminating the impact that they have on your life and relationships.

Relationships are not fair

WHEN IT COMES TO RELATIONSHIPS, we don't always get out of them what we put into them. Sadly, they are not always fair. Over the years, I have had clients say to me, 'But I gave him everything he asked for and didn't ask for. Why doesn't he return my love?' The answer to this question is complicated, messy, and imperfect. People are not always what they seem. Sometimes kindness can be taken for granted. Sometimes our kindness or help is just not needed.

We discover quickly that life isn't fair, and the same is true for relationships. Just because you *like* people's social media posts doesn't mean that other people will do the same. Just because you value birthdays and like to give surprises doesn't mean that other people have the same values.

Jenna was 34 years old at the time of her visit with me. She had been in a relationship with her partner for two years. Jenna came from a family who loved to celebrate birthdays and other holidays. Jenna thoroughly enjoyed organizing celebrations for other people and could not understand why her partner or anyone else wouldn't enjoy celebrations. She firmly believed that celebrations and gifts were a major way of showing love for other people. One of Jenna's top love languages was gifts. Jenna's partner came from a family where they were affirmative and encouraging. They often told each other how much they loved each other. They often verbalized appreciation and gratitude. Words of affirmation was a high priority love language in their family, not gifts.

Jenna became mindful that she and her partner spoke different love languages. Their show of love may not look reciprocal. Just because she threw her partner a surprise 35th birthday party doesn't mean that he will do the same for her next year when she turns 35. Communication is paramount.

Jenna increased her awareness of the need to talk to her partner about what she wanted for her 35th birthday instead of assuming her partner would 'know' to reciprocate and surprise her with something big.

Unconditional love

I HAVE KNOWN NO LOVE greater than the love I had for my newborn children. No strings attached. No conditions. No reciprocity.

Romantic love comes with conditions and strings attached. Romantic love needs some type of reciprocity for it to blossom. In the beginning, romantic love is playful, youthful, and joyful. Most people hope that romantic love will progress into mature, stable, and consistent love.

Many of us are confused by the concept of mature love. Mature love isn't necessarily unconditional, passionate, and fun. Mature love is work. Mature love consists of being intentional about keeping the fire lit and experiencing pleasure.

Mature relationships aren't always peaches and cream.

AFTER BEING IN A STABLE, cohabiting relationship for several years, it is challenging for Martha to look at Frank every day and think loving and positive thoughts. Some days, she may wonder what life would be like if she weren't in this long-term relationship. As long as Martha doesn't entertain or act on this unwelcome thought, then it can be harmless.

When we are in mature, long-term relationships, we often experience emotions that vacillate from satisfaction to dissatisfaction, happiness to sadness, joy to pain, and fun to boredom. Mature relationships aren't always *peaches and cream*. If the good outweighs the bad, the relationship can continue to stand the test of time. If we get lost in desiring passion and action in our relationship, then we might not be ready for mature love. Be mindful of whether you are ready for a mature relationship that has bumps, bruises, fun, boredom, passion, and lulls.

Being mindful of not being ready for a mature relationship is not a bad thing. It's just a thing! Mindful Acceptance encourages us to be mindful of our reality, self-compassionate about what has been brought to our awareness, intentional about being non-judgmental, and creative in finding new life in the relationship. Be mindful that realities are not static and can change.

ROMANTIC LOVE CAN BECOME a neurotic sense of attachment, which some people can mistake for unconditional love. Lauren was a 28-year-old single woman who had moved around from foster home to foster home beginning at 4 years old. Lauren was never adopted.

Lauren had been dating Paul on and off for about one year. She thought that she loved Paul with all her heart. Lauren then found out that Paul had been unfaithful to her on numerous occasions within the first couple of months of the relationship. She was determined not to leave Paul because of her love for him. She even blamed herself for Paul's unfaithfulness. Lauren tried to be a better partner by having more sex with him and giving in to more of his requests. Secretly, she feared that Paul would abandon her like everyone else.

Lauren did not hold Paul accountable for his infidelity, and she acted as if it never happened. She was not living in reality! The reality was that Paul didn't love her the way that she wanted to be loved. Lauren's love for Paul might have been immature and unhealthy. Lauren had not healed from her childhood fear of abandonment. She needed to be mindful of her personal reality, self-compassionate towards her suffering and pain, intentional about managing thoughts related to abandonment, and creative about discovering more constructive behaviors.

Being nice

EVEN NICE PEOPLE WANT SOMETHING in return. Be aware of people who are too nice. They say they want nothing from you, but they often do. A woman who is too nice may want you to commit to a relationship with her. A friend who is too nice may be preparing you for a big favor.

Suppose that Samantha and Nora are friends who have known each other for a little under one year. Samantha is very ingratiating. She latches on to Nora quickly and tries to monopolize her time. Samantha offers to pick Nora up for parties and refuses gas money. Samantha pet sits at Nora's home free of charge. Nora thinks Samantha is tolerable to have around given that she seems easy going and people-pleasing. However, she can be quite annoying because she doesn't seem to have a mind of her own. Samantha just agrees with Nora and does whatever Nora wants.

One day, out of the blue, Samantha asks Nora for a favor that Nora perceives as big. She wants to borrow Nora's spare car while her car is in the shop being repaired. Samantha did not want to pay for a rental car. She figured that if Nora were in the same situation, she would offer for her to use her car. Samantha thought, 'Why would it be an issue if I asked to borrow her car?' Samantha does just that. She asks Nora to borrow her spare car.

What would you do in this situation if you were Nora and didn't feel comfortable allowing anyone who was not on your insurance to drive your car? Nora considers herself a rather rational person, and allowing someone to drive her car who was not on her insurance just didn't sit well with her.

Again, what do you do? Samantha has always been there for you, even when you neither asked nor wanted her to be there. At the same time, you did not refuse her assistance. Your mind makes you feel guilty about wanting to say no by nagging and saying, 'How could you possibly tell her no? Wouldn't this make you a bad person?' You do not think Samantha's ingratiating behavior was nefarious or malicious. You and Samantha might have a different view of how friendships work. Samantha views friendships without boundaries while you might view friendships with boundaries.

In this situation, Nora may want to consider being mindful of how she landed in this situation. She can increase awareness that she allowed Samantha to do things for her that she could have done herself. Nora needs to provide compassion to herself for her current predicament. She may want to consider being intentional about her current and future dealings with Samantha. In this situation, Nora needs to be intentional about engaging in value-driven behavior, such as telling Samantha that she is uncomfortable with allowing her to borrow her car because she had been burned in the past by allowing

THE FOUR DISCIPLINES OF ROMANCE

non-insured persons to drive her car. Nora can provide compassion to herself by intentionally telling herself that saying no does not make her a bad person given that she is often warm and kind.

If we are overly nice to others, we need to question our own motives. What do we want in return? Are we genuinely nice to other people because it feels good to us or do we secretly want something in return from them, maybe loyalty? Researchers have found that altruistic behavior makes us feel good. For instance, research by Harvard Behavior School professor Michael I. Norton and colleagues Elizabeth W. Dunn and Lara B. Aknin found that giving people money increased the giver's happiness more than spending money on herself.

What do we expect from the other person if we are nice to them? Does the other person know our expectations? If we are unaware of why we are ingratiating, we may end up angry and resentful. What typically happens is that the other person takes us for granted and begins to expect special treatment without having to do anything in return. It is up to us to accept the reality that other people are not mind readers and will not put energy into figuring out our wants and needs.

Denial can be toxic

WE CAN ONLY DENY THE REALITY of a relationship for so long before it smacks us in the face, sometimes literally. Claire was a beautiful 30-year-old single parent. When we first talked, she had just ended an abusive 13-month relationship that lasted far too long. Within a few months of her relationship, she reported that her partner grabbed her so roughly by her arms that she had a visible bruise. She told herself it was not a big deal because he did not strike or punch her. Claire was in denial about the aggression in her relationship.

Six months into the relationship, Claire and her partner were engaged in a heated argument over something petty. Claire was pushed and knocked over the sofa. Her partner even punched a hole into the wall. Claire made excuses for her partner saying that he was typically a kind and awesome person; maybe *she* triggered his anger. She began to engage in destructive self-talk, imagining that if her partner would just see a therapist, his anger issues would go away.

Claire had been engaging in two sneaky forms of denial. The first was her slanted thinking about the nature of her partner's past behavior. The second was the false hope concerning her partner's future behavior. These two types of denial prevented Claire from truly affirming and understanding her present reality. Unfortunately, Claire was listening to her thoughts of fear and loneliness, which prevented her from clearly seeing the situation and making safe decisions.

Claire's situation became progressively worse. Her partner did eventually strike her, which made it impossible for her to deny her situation any longer. Upon release from the hospital, Claire sought therapy and began treatment to work on developing a healthier relationship with herself in order to prevent being caught up in another abusive relationship. Claire implemented Mindful Acceptance in her life by utilizing mindfulness exercises to help her snap out of autopilot and become intentional about making decisions that acknowledged what mattered most to her, such as her self-respect, safety, and emotional health.

Leaving an unhealthy relationship

MANY OF US REMAIN IN UNHEALTHY RELATIONSHIPS because we are hoping, wishing, and praying that the other person will change. I hate to be the bearer of bad news, but putting energy into praying that a person will change is a big mistake! Admittedly, I am a praying person, and I believe that prayer can change things. At the same time, life has shown me that if you want to use your prayers and emotional energy wisely, you might want to consider putting more energy into praying for your strength to make positive decisions that are in your best interest rather than in praying for someone else to change. No one knows how long it will take for the prayer to work at changing another person. Praying for oneself to change and believing in it has proven, immediate results. This is not to say that praying for other people is not helpful. Pray for other people; pray for the world. Don't stop praying. Make healthy decisions based on your current reality and values, not on whom a person may become after prayer changes them.

Be intentional about your prayers, especially in relationships. Instead of praying for my partner to change and fit my expectation of a perfect partner, I pray for myself to be more loving and less critical. I pray for strength to look for the good in him. This type of prayer has real, proven, and effective results.

If you are in a relationship where you experience more negative situations than positive situations, then you need to ask yourself honestly:

- What is the status of my current relationship?
- Are we committed or casual?
- How am I being treated?
- Is this the reality that I envision for my future?
- Is my behavior aligned with my values?

Answering these questions candidly will help you become more aware of your true situation. Accepting the reality of 'what is' today, not what it was when you first met or what it could be tomorrow, will prevent you from being involved in unhealthy situations such as domestic violence or emotional abuse. By honestly looking at the reality of your relationship, you will be showing respect and love to yourself.

WE NEED TO COMMIT TO FIGURING OUT how to change ourselves rather than trying to change other people. Xavier and Sue were a really cute, comical, and lovely couple who had recently moved in together by the time they came to visit me. Xavier had a history of depression and cognitive limitations. Sue criticized Xavier for not handling things the way he was *supposed* to handle them. Xavier did not help with the children the way he *should* help with them. Interestingly, Xavier attempted to get the children prepared for school, pick them up, and prepare dinner the way Sue wanted him to, but nothing was ever good enough. She didn't think he picked them up from aftercare early enough, and she nagged that the meals he prepared were not nutritious. Sue took it upon herself to take over the management of the children, house, and financials.

Sue blamed Xavier for their relationship difficulties because she thought that he could not do anything right. Because of Xavier's inability to do things the right way (that is, her way), she *had* to do everything herself. Sue was tired and overwhelmed.

Unless Sue dealt with her peculiarities about how things *should* be done, they would be in a no-win situation, because it wasn't about Xavier as much as it was about Sue's control issues. After we identified this never-ending cycle, we concluded that Sue and Xavier had to determine if the situation was a deal breaker, a perpetual problem, or an opportunity for the couple to change, grow, or stretch.

Xavier and Sue discovered that their relationship values were very dissimilar. Sue said that it was necessary that she had a helpmate, and she did not feel that Xavier was able to meet her need. Given that Sue acknowledged that Xavier was unable to meet her standards, acceptance of his limitations was explored. Sue was unable to accept that he was doing the best he could do; therefore, she continued to struggle with his lack of help. Xavier said that it was essential for him to have a supportive and understanding mate, and Sue wasn't showing compassion for his attempts to help. Not every couple has a happily ever after. This couple continued to struggle because they were unwilling to make room and accommodations for the reality of their individual differences.

Accepting loving gestures

I'M ALWAYS BAFFLED when someone says, 'I want him to *want* to do something. In the very funny 2006 movie, *The Break-Up*, the leading actress griped to her friend about her partner saying, 'I want him to want to do the dishes,' and, 'I want him to want to take me to the ballet.'

Let's not waste a lot of mental energy complaining about wanting to control someone else's wants and desires. Be grateful when a person wants to please you even if they don't necessarily desire to engage in a particular behavior. We don't have a lot of control over our desires. I don't necessarily desire to watch Star Wars movies and other sci-fi flicks that my partner enjoys. My desire to please him is genuine, and that is what is most important.

Interestingly, Heather Patrick, a research assistant professor at the University of Rochester, found that when we engage in sacrifices for our partner because we genuinely want to, and not because we are coerced or obligated, we are more satisfied in our relationships. She found that the partner who perceived that her mate did something for her genuinely has similarly satisfying relationships.

It's up to you how you choose to perceive your partner's gesture. If your partner agrees to take you to the ballet, do you refuse because you know that he really doesn't want to go?

Or, do you perceive this as a positive sacrifice that your partner is willing to make in the interest of pleasing you? Patrick's research confirms that couples are more committed and satisfied in relationships that affirm these genuine sacrifices.

Be mindful and intentional about informing your partner what pleases you so that he can make an informed decision about contributing to your happiness. Healthy relationships strive when *both parties* know what the other wants and needs and enjoys pleasing the other person. I've heard my husband jokingly say to other men, 'Happy wife, happy life!' I must say that I do concur. My husband knows what makes me happy because I tell him.

It is unhealthy to be untruthful or ambiguous about what you want and need from a relationship. For all the strong, independent people out there: Please do not say that you don't want anything from the other person because that is exactly what you will get. As the saying goes, 'You have not because you ask not.'

When words and actions don't match

OVER THE YEARS, I HAVE SAT WITH many clients who have dealt with situations in which their partner's words and actions did not match. For example, James tells Lacy that he is not ready to be in a committed relationship, but he spends time with her, and they continue to engage in physical intimacy. The hardcore reality is that James is not ready to commit and it is Lacy's choice to be in a 'friends with benefits' relationship with him or not. If Lacy is holding on to the fantasy that somehow, he will eventually see her as a life partner, then she is in denial concerning her role in the relationship and resisting reality.

Lacy's current relationship does not appear to help her function as her Best Self. If we ask Lacy how does she feel, she may say, 'I am sad.' When asked why she is sad, she may say, 'Because James continues to treat me unfairly.' If asked what would take her sadness away, she may respond, 'I will be happy when James realizes my worth and begins to treat me like a queen.' In this situation, Lacy has given James responsibility for her emotional wellness and the power to control her emotions and subsequent behaviors. Lacy can practice living as her Best Self by no longer allowing her happiness or behaviors to be contingent on what James says or does.

MANY OF US CONTINUE TO be in a relationship with a person who has consistently demonstrated conflicting and inconsistent behavior. The sooner we acknowledge the reality of the situation, the happier we will be. Be mindful that while we can't control whom we love or desire, we can control our behavior. We can choose whether we will be someone's doormat. We can become more aware of unhealthy situations and emotionally strong enough to leave when our love isn't reciprocated.

If you don't like your role in a relationship, it may be time to get out of it. Arguing and fussing with your 'friend' about how he doesn't take you out on dates or introduce you to his friends will not change the situation. Don't sit around waiting on the other person to change. We must accept and take responsibility for our lives and emotional health. This means that we do what is in our best interest and refuse to suffocate in relationships that are unhealthy or unfulfilling.

Best Self in Action: Relationship reality check

MANY PEOPLE CAN BENEFIT FROM a reality check of their relationships. The situations briefly described below indicate a few cases that call for changes in a relationship. Can you relate to any of these people?

- Lisa's romantic friend typically calls her after 10pm to 'hang out or kick it.' She may be a 'booty call.'
- Carmen and Luke tend to sweep situations under the rug until one of them explodes. They may have communication difficulties that need to be addressed.

- Allison and her mother-in-law bump heads about core values. They may never be best friends, but instead, there is hope that they could be cordial and co-exist.

Once you are able to clearly see what is occurring in your relationships, you are then able to make intentional, informed, and healthy decisions that have your best interest at heart. Practice going through the day with full awareness of the nature of your relationships.

13

Mind Reading

I CANNOT TELL YOU HOW MANY TIMES I have sat with a frustrated individual who complained that her partner should have known what she needed. I have sat in couple's counseling sessions with a very agitated man yelling at his partner about what she *should* have known about him. I completely disagree! My clients have heard me say this repeatedly: there is no way our partners can know exactly what we want or need. We are responsible for sharing our wants and needs with our partner. We are responsible for sharing our vulnerabilities, sensitivities, and mental knots with our partner so that he might be able to share in our healing and growth. *Mind reading is simply not possible, even if our partner has known us for years.*

Mind reading is the cognitive or mental process where we assume we know what other people think and feel. In the same breath, we think other people *should* know what we feel and think. Mind reading is a major cognitive barrier to effective communication because we may be reluctant to check in with the other person if we think that we already know what he is thinking and feeling.

Making gentle assumptions

ONLINE DATING HAS ALMOST REPLACED traditional, meet at the coffee shop dating. Given that the popularity of online dating is relatively new, the rules are unclear. This is a situation where it would be really risky to assume that you know anything about the other person. When in doubt, *ask, ask, ask.* Don't assume that because a person doesn't say that they have children, that they don't have them. Ask the person on the other side of cyber world, 'Do you have children?'

No one talks on the phone anymore. Everyone texts. Don't assume that other people know that you don't like texting and you find it rude. Tell people that you would prefer to talk on the phone. What about when you call someone and they text you back instead of answering the phone or returning the call? If you think that is rude, tell the other person!

We are practicing emotional self-care when we learn to let go of trying to figure out what someone meant by an email, text, or comment. Much cognitive energy, time, and effort are exhausted when we are evaluating ambiguous messages. Unless we ask the other person what he meant, we may never know the real reason why something was done or said. Even when we ask people why something was said or done, we may not get a satisfactory answer. We have to make space for situations that we do not understand. Refuse to create a story that cannot be fact checked. Learn to sit with ambiguity. Pause, breathe, and let go.

Stories that work for us

IN INTIMATE RELATIONSHIPS, we take for granted what our partner knows about us. Avery and Joe have known each other for approximately three years but have been in a committed relationship for one year. They had a disagreement that occurred over the past weekend, which left both of them feeling 'some type of way.'

Joe was known to easily brush things off while Avery was prone to holding on to anger. Later that night, after the disagreement, Avery was stewing and pouting about their recent argument. She created an elaborate story in her head about what she expected him to say to her given that she was clearly displaying frustration. Avery's thinking that Joe *should* know how to respond and the fact that he was not responding the way that she wanted him was causing significant distress for her. Avery desperately wanted Joe to gently say, 'I know that you are still frustrated about our conversation earlier. I am here for you, and I want to talk about it when you are ready.' He was oblivious that she thought that he would know to say those things and in the gentle tone. Instead of Avery informing Joe of her needs, in that pivotal moment, she refused to communicate with Joe about how she was feeling. Joe asked her what was the matter. She said, 'Nothing.' Clearly something was wrong. Joe did his part by attempting to communicate. Avery will need to be mindful of taking care of her needs and asking for what she wants instead of assuming Joe would intuitively know how to soothe her.

HAVE YOU EVER BEEN FRUSTRATED because you thought that someone who knows you personally *should* have known something about you? Imagine that Robert has been working for five years in corporate America and a higher-level position becomes available. Robert cannot directly apply for this position. He has to be referred by his immediate supervisor. Robert is interested in this position, but he does not mention it to his immediate supervisor who is his friend, because he felt that she *should* know that he is interested.

Robert creates a story about how his supervisor *should* ask him to apply for the job. Robert's story goes something like this: 'My supervisor knows that I want to move up in the company, we are good friends, and she wants me to win. I will wait for her to mention this position to me, because if I mention it to her, it might look like I am just her friend to get something out of her.'

Unfortunately, Robert does not mention his interest in this job, and she never offers it to him. Initially, Robert is livid with his supervisor and blames her for not mentioning the job to him. Robert can do himself a big favor by refusing to blame anyone for the outcome of the situation. He could practice living as his Best Self by considering how might he behave differently if another opportunity comes around.

I ONCE OVERHEARD A BRIDE VENTING about what her bridal party and future in-laws *should* know. In the bride's head, she thought that any idiot who has ever been a part of a wedding *should* know to meet in the wedding hall at least an hour before showtime. She did not clearly inform people of what she wanted and needed because she thought that they *should* have known. The bride was livid. She was in tears and emotionally aroused. Unfortunately, this bride was unable to enjoy her special day. She was so frustrated that she was missing precious moments that would never be returned to her. This was her first marriage, and she would never get the opportunity to redo these missed moments, which could have been magical. Failed mind reading can steal our peace and joy.

Being your own advocate

SANDY HAD BEEN MARRIED TO BOB for six years, and her stepson was 9 years old when she first visited me. Sandy had to deal with *baby mama drama* because her stepson's biological mother, Haley, didn't seem to respect her marriage. Haley would call Bob late at night under the guise of co-parenting. Haley continued to remain in contact with Bob's family. Occasionally, she had shown up uninvited at family events. For years, Sandy didn't say anything to Bob about this or other situations that she thought were disrespectful. She used to think that they all *should* know better and things would eventually change. Well, things did change, but not for the better. Sandy became increasingly anxious and depressed. Haley's boundary pushing increased until Sandy couldn't take it anymore, and she had several epic fights with Bob. Eventually, she came to see me.

Sandy could not understand why she exploded on Bob. She couldn't stop complaining about his relationship with Haley. Sandy admitted that on the day of their first fight, she dumped everything on him that had been building up inside her for years. Bob felt attacked, so he attacked back. Sandy really wanted to be validated in how she perceived her current situation. Bob was unable to validate her experience because he was in defense mode.

When people don't express their disagreement about something, they are sending the message that they agree with it. How would the other person know that you don't like something if you don't tell her? Do you expect others to just know that they *should* or *should* not be doing something? If we do not tell people what bothers us, then we cannot hold them accountable for getting on our nerves.

Sandy learned about Mindful Acceptance and mindful communication. She increased her awareness of the concept of *silence implies consent*. She practiced compassion about all the pastimes in which she thought that she *should* have spoken up about something. Sandy was encouraged to be kind to herself for the fear of confrontation that she experienced throughout her life because she wasn't allowed to have a voice in her childhood.

If you don't tell someone that she has offended or bothered you, that becomes your private issue that will fester inside you. When you inform a person of what you don't like and he continues to engage in bothersome behaviors, then it becomes a real concern that both of you can discuss openly and honestly.

Other people are not an extension of us. They have not experienced what we have in life; there is no way they can know what we are thinking. We must express ourselves. Expressing ourselves does not mean dropping hints; it means saying exactly what we want and need. If we have expressed ourselves, and other people still choose not to do as requested, then we have some choices to make. Rather than getting frustrated about something that did not happen, we can choose to accept that something did not happen and figure out a way to do it ourselves. Or, we can choose on what level and in what capacity we want to relate to the person who is not respecting our requests.

I choose to take responsibility for my wants and needs and do not expect someone to read my mind, regardless of how long we have known each other. If I have not expressed my concerns or needs to another person, then I do not become angry with them for not behaving how I think they should behave. I don't blame anyone; I take responsibility for not expressing myself and vow to do a better job of expressing myself in the future.

There are several tools for managing mind reading. Being mindful and compassionate are good places to begin because we all engage in mind reading from time to time. We first identify the thoughts that assume we know what is going on with the other person or the thoughts where we assume that the other person *should* know what is going on with us. We can hold our mind reading stories lightly and choose not to get caught up in them. We can engage in a variety of ways to test our assumptions. Mind reading is not inherently bad; it is just problematic if we are not backing up our assumptions with evidence. One way that we can test our assumption is by fact checking with the other person. If a friend doesn't call us back when she says she will, we may automatically think that she doesn't want to talk to us. Your friend might have had a lot going on and didn't get around to calling you back. The next time you talk to your friend, ask her if everything is good with you guys, and inform her that you are concerned because she didn't return your call the other night. This might open the door for communication if something truly is wrong or this might highlight the distortion in your mind reading thought.

A caveat is that we cannot make people communicate with us or be honest. We have to rely on other sources to test our assumptions. It is helpful to ask ourselves, 'What is the evidence for and against our assumptions?' This is where we allow ourselves to honestly observe the current and past behavior of our friend and experience.

SOPHIA HAD WHAT SHE THOUGHT was a close girlfriend. They appeared to enjoy each other's company and have fun together. Their children were the same age, and they did family activities together. Over time, Sophia's friend seemed increasingly unavailable, so she stopped inviting her to activities and events.

As more time passed, Sophia and her friend slowly drifted apart. The dwindling friendship bothered Sophia, so she decided to talk to her friend about their distancing relationship. Sophia wanted to know where they went awry and if she did something wrong. Sophia's friend said that nothing happened; she was just busy. Well, Sophia took this information at face value. *It is what it is!*

Sophia tried on at least two occasions to communicate, but it flopped. At that point, Sophia had to count her losses and move on. Sophia thought, 'There are no harsh feelings, because, maybe as my former friend said, she is just busy.' Sophia had to make emotional room and sit with the unknown of that situation. She had to refuse to get caught up in stories for which she had no way of checking the evidence.

Best Self in Action: Letting go of anger

ANGER IS AN INTERESTING EMOTION that has a bad rap. Anger is not inherently problematic. It is adaptive and helpful in increasing our awareness of external events happening around us. Anger can motivate us to engage in social justice and other constructive activities. Holding on to anger and getting caught up in irrational thoughts, such as *should* thinking, is problematic. Consider the following scenarios:

- Jackie is angry because she thinks she *should* not have to tell her partner to clean up behind himself because it is common courtesy.

- Trevor believes that he *should* not have to tell his girl-friend that he doesn't like it when he tells her about a conflict that he had with someone else and she supports the other person.

- Cathy is convinced that she *should* not have to tell her spouse that she needs help with the children.

- Mason is emotionally exhausted because he thinks he *should* not have to tell his partner that he does not like spending time around large groups of people.

- Aaron is frustrated because he *should* not have to tell his brother that it bothers him when he criticizes him in front of their friends.

If any of these situations resonate with you, please be mindful of thinking that other people can read your mind and *should* know what you want and need. It is your responsibility to clearly express yourself. What if you express yourself and the other person still does not do what you want or stop doing something? Practice taking responsibility for your happiness by prioritizing your needs, letting go of trying to change someone, or removing yourself from toxic situations.

14

BEING COMFORTABLE
WITH CHANGE

MINDFUL ACCEPTANCE INCLUDES being aware of, acknowledging, and accepting the imperfections of life while taking care of and honoring ourselves. Very rarely will we feel that our life is in perfect harmony. It usually doesn't take long before we begin to notice that these seemingly perfect events begin to lose their luster. The honeymoon phase of a marriage eventually ends. The newborn child isn't predictable and won't sleep through the night. Many new graduates encounter the unsettling reality of the job market. We have to be mindful, intentional, self-compassionate, and creative about respecting the imperfections of life without getting stuck in its struggle.

It is easy to notice the perfect harmony of nature such as the day and night taking turns to wake us up and put us to sleep. There doesn't seem to be competition and domination between the sun and moon. It is quite amazing to spot the moon in the sky before the sun has completely set. As part of my practice of Mindful Acceptance, I allow this phenomenon to put me in a space of perfect harmony.

It is not as easy to notice the perfect harmony of imperfections. Imperfections make us human. With that being said, imperfections allow us to experience compassion for other humans. We all have imperfections whether we want to admit it or not. This shared reality is one of the many bonds that connect humans from around the globe.

In relationships, seasons change.

PEOPLE COME INTO OUR LIVES FOR A REASON, season, and if we are truly blessed, for a lifetime. When a relationship becomes unhealthy or someone wants to leave, be comfortable with saying good-bye and closing those chapters in life. Seasons in life will come to a natural end. It's ok to mourn the past. Just don't get stuck in it. Be grateful for the lessons taught and growth that might have occurred, and move forward without grudges or baggage. Increase Mindful Acceptance and engage in emotional self-care when a relationship ends. Accept without labeling, judging, or criticizing your Self about what happened in the relationship. Do not try to force it to be something that it is not. Compassionately comfort your Self for this loss and prepare to make wise decisions that will have lasting positive effects.

Natalie and Mila had been close friends since undergraduate college years. Upon graduation, they moved to different states and didn't communicate as often. Natalie got married shortly after college and began having children. Mila remained single and enjoyed the dating life. A very significant relationship appeared to be changing. The two women's lives were going in different directions; they didn't have as much in common anymore. Natalie felt like she was losing her best friend. Instead of Natalie holding on to the way things used to be and becoming frustrated because things were different, she graciously decided to walk into a new season with her friend. The new season included occasional texts and social media communication. The new season was nothing like the old season. Natalie respected the relationship that she had with Mila and became open to creating a new relationship with her that took into consideration their current locations, lifestyles, and careers. They have a friendship that has now weathered several seasons.

Seasons change. If you lose your job and know that you were a hard worker and did the best that you could do, then apparently, the season has changed for your employment. The same goes true for relationships. If you know that you did the best that you could in a relationship and it still doesn't work out, let it go, because it might not be for you. Accept without self-criticism or judgment that this season is changing. Allow self-compassion to guide you into making wise decisions about your future. If you effectively let go of seasons that have passed, don't be surprised if your new work season or new love life is better than the last.

Representatives of the Self

WE ALL HAVE AN INNER REPRESENTATIVE or specific self who works hard at putting our best foot forward and trying to be impressive. Over time, our representative will step back, revealing our whole Self in all its glory. This is why it is imperative not to rush into relationships. Time will reveal all aspects of the person.

Couples often complain, 'We are just so different.' My initial response is, 'Well, what attracted you to the other person?' Typically, the response is, 'Initially, we did everything together and had so much in common.' When we first meet someone, we are typically not meeting the real person, but one representative of the whole person.

Dylan and Nicole met online. It was love at first picture. Nicole lived in the United States while Dylan lived in a poor country in the Caribbean. Nicole went to visit Dylan, and she was attracted to how generous he was, even though his family did not have much money. While she was visiting, he made sure that Nicole had everything that she needed. Nicole's impression of Dylan was that he would have given her the shirt off his back for her to be comfortable. Shortly after, Dylan moved to the United States with Nicole. He was no longer the generous and altruistic man that Nicole met. Dylan became selfish, stingy, and possessive. His ability to maintain this façade had ended and he was revealing more of himself. Nicole's knight had no shining armor. Unfortunately, Dylan and Nicole split up shortly after Nicole helped him moved to the States.

Many relationships end when couples have to work at getting along, having fun, and remaining passionate. Mature relationships have to be nurtured and cultivated in order to continue to grow. Mature love is not always fun because sometimes couples have to agree to disagree, bite the bullet, assert themselves in uncomfortable situations, and extend and receive forgiveness. Mature love forces you to create a healthy and meaningful partnership with your lover.

When opposites attract

PEOPLE ARE OFTEN COMPATIBLE WITH LOVERS who have opposite temperaments and interests. For example, I worked with a vibrant and youthful couple: Andrew and Leah. Andrew described himself as an introvert with an easy temperament. He was not easily moved or agitated. He was functioning as his Best Self when he was engaging in solo activities such as gardening or sculpting. His preference was to be home with his family rather than socializing with groups of people whom he might not know well. His wife, Leah, described herself as an extravert with a more aggressive style of dealing with things. Leah is energized when she is with other people. If she had a problem, she would rather talk to someone about it than to deal with it alone.

Leah and Andrew met in college. Leah was attracted to him because he appeared to be a good listener and he wasn't 'on the party scene.' Although Leah did not want to date a party person, she did enjoy partying. Leah just did not want a partner who enjoyed it as much as she did. Andrew didn't seem to compete with her for attention when they would hang out with other people. Andrew's isolation allowed Leah to do her thing and work the room. Over time, Leah began to resent Andrew, seeing his introversion as a weakness.

Before practicing Mindful Acceptance, Leah was easily angered, agitated, and annoyed when Andrew didn't do what she wanted him to do, especially when it came to interacting and socializing with people the way she thought he *should*.

Leah would attempt to make Andrew feel defective by suggesting that something was wrong with him for not wanting to mingle with large groups of people.

The skills of Mindful Acceptance prevented Leah from becoming too agitated and sharp-tongued with Andrew for being a homebody. Although Leah continued to become agitated at times when she wanted to attend social functions but Andrew did not want to, she realized that the agitation was her issue and not Andrew's. This awareness helped Leah to check herself and emotionally recompose.

Leah realized that she could still attend social functions without Andrew if she really wanted to attend. She increased her awareness of the thoughts coming to her head about attending these events alone such as:

- I wonder what will other people think of me being alone?
- I wonder will they think Andrew and I are separated?
- I wonder if I will look silly?

Leah was intentional about not getting hooked by the thoughts in her head and allowing them to prevent her from engaging in an activity that she enjoyed.

Once Leah took the undue pressure off Andrew, he wanted to attend more social functions with Leah because he wasn't feeling controlled. He wanted to make her happy. Because they valued showing love and respect for each other, they were willing to compromise to meet the other's needs without denying their own needs. Similarly, Leah realized that she and Andrew balanced each other. His mellow temperament helped Leah *turn down* when she was ready to *turn up*, especially in disagreements. Leah and Andrew learned how to incorporate the principles of Mindful Acceptance in their marriage, and they went on to love each other passionately without reservations.

On getting along

DIFFERENT PERSONALITY TYPES, STYLES, AND WAYS of doing things don't mean that we are incompatible. If we are receptive and open, our partner's opposite style could balance and complement us.

Doug and Lynn were professionals in their early 40's. They were newlyweds at the time they came to visit me. Their concern was communication difficulties. Like most couples, their issues were much deeper. Lynn was an outspoken, outgoing, and driven lady. Doug was a relatively mellow, easy going, and agreeable man. Their conflict was especially contrasted in areas of punctuality, cleanliness, and spontaneity. Lynn was meticulous, organized, and traditional, while Doug was relaxed, somewhat disorganized, and spontaneous.

Interestingly, Doug planned a surprise vacation for Lynn. Much to Doug's dismay, Lynn was not very receptive of this surprise. Lynn was infuriated when she found out on a Wednesday that she would be going out of town on that Friday. The week prior, Doug had already confirmed with Lynn that they did not have weekend plans.

Doug did not realize how important planning was to Lynn. Doug would have loved for someone to plan a spontaneous getaway for him. Doug began to realize that he and Lynn functioned in the world differently. The couple discussed several other situations in which they could respect and appreciate their differences. Lynn was very organized and tidy, which meant that Doug did not have to worry about managing the house or planning for family events. Given that Doug was rather low maintenance, Lynn was allowed to be herself without a lot of protest from him.

Lynn and Doug's opposite way of relating in the world can be perceived as complementary instead of opposite. *It is up to them* to focus on how they complement each other instead of on how they are opposite. Focusing on the former will increase Lynn and Doug's relationship satisfaction. Acceptance of complementary traits was a major focus of counseling with Lynn and Doug.

Lynn's tidiness and organization appeared to be controlling and rigid. She demonstrated behaviors of mild obsessive-compulsive disorder about certain things, such as keeping blinds closed, turning lights off when not in use, and closing doors when vacant. These seemingly minor infractions would send Lynn in overdrive, and she would argue with Doug over these behaviors. Lynn's rigidity became too much for Doug. She was unwilling or unable at the moment to let go of controlling behaviors to make her partnership work. The practice of Mindful Acceptance leads us out of relationships that don't give us what we need.

Finding your sweet spot

SCARLETT, A SINGLE MOTHER OF YOUNG CHILDREN who works long hours outside the home may want the same opportunities for her children as the child from the two-parent, two-income home. Understandably so! Scarlett compares her situation to other situations that are not comparable. It is difficult to compare apples to apples in these situations.

Where is the balance between Scarlett's work and family? It doesn't exist. An equal distribution of time between work and family obligations will almost never be accomplished. A proposed solution is to increase awareness of the lack of balance and engage in behaviors that make sense for her and her family given her current situation. Scarlett may need to find out which arrangement of distribution of time would provide the most harmony to her life, which would be her unique personal balance that does not require equal distributions of time. It will be helpful for her to be mindful of her current situation and reality, self-compassionate about what's been brought to her awareness, intentional about not comparing her situations to others, and creative about figuring out what might work for her family.

'Balance is a myth. Harmony is a must.'
— Lisa Nichols

CONSIDER EVA, AN ENTREPRENEUR who is working long hours in an attempt to get a business up and running. How does she satisfy her professional goals and her need to be in a healthy relationship with her current partner? Eva can be mindful that no relationship or business situation is perfect. She can find her unique personal balance, or sweet spot, and that doesn't mean an equal distribution of time. For Eva, achieving harmony is what makes sense to her with her current circumstances. Eva can be mindful of the importance of communication and intentional about having a plan and expressing it to her partner. She can be creative about finding time for her and her partner to spend together. She can be self-compassionate for the many times she chooses to work instead of spending time with her partner.

Best Self in Action: Letting go

FOR MANY PEOPLE, LETTING GO can be difficult. Fears of change, abandonment, and ambiguity are a few reasons people struggle with letting go. For other people, they seem to have a gift of letting go. Regardless to whether you appear to have a gift or not, it is definitely a healthy skill to have when used flexibly. Practice letting go of beliefs, people, places, and things that are not working for you.

- William resisted leaving a job that did not appear to have upward mobility or purpose.
- Tracy was frustrated with her partner because their relationship changed after several years of being together.
- June resisted her son changing from dependent and clingy to independent and resistant.
- Bailey struggled with the flip side of being grown and living away from her childhood home.
- Kiley struggled with challenging her childhood religious beliefs.

Be mindful that there is always a flip side to life and that all things eventually change. Time doesn't stop for anyone, and change is inevitable. Relationships change, we change, other people change, and situations change. As the saying goes, everything changes, so don't take it personally. Practice enjoying your current reality while it exists, but be mindful and aware that nothing stays the same.

15

MANAGING FEAR-BASED THINKING

FEAR, IF UNMANAGED, MAY HINDER emotional growth by preventing us from standing up for our values, asking for what we want, or removing ourselves from an unhealthy situation. Fear can prevent us from even attempting to achieve our goals, lowering our self-confidence.

The emotion of fear elicits *biological* stress responses such as increased blood flow, blood pressure, and heart rate to give the body increased strength and speed in anticipation of fight, flight, or freeze responses. These physiological responses are stored in the primitive parts of our brain and are adaptive and evolutionary. These emotions have been with humans since the beginning of our existence. Even now, if you are in the woods and you see a black bear, your body will respond instinctively. Your adaptive, evolutionary response to fight, run, or stand still will take over to ensure your survival. Over time, other parts of the human brain began to develop, which allowed us to use judgment and reason. The physiological responses in our brain never changed when other parts of our brain were developed. We still have the primitive responses of fight, flight, or freeze, which help us when we encounter real danger. We have the same stress responses when we fear imagined, anticipated, and unfounded danger.

The emotion of fear triggers psychological stress responses such as negative thoughts of danger and doom: *I'm going to die. I don't know what to do. I won't make it out of this.* This psychological stress response to fear could become maladaptive because it may lead to more complicated forms of fear such as anxiety and phobia. Anxiety is an extreme form of fear that is an anticipation of danger. People who struggle with anxiety fear the anticipation of a future threat. A phobia is extreme fear about a specific object or situation. There is a phobia for almost any fear. Have you encountered anyone who appears to have ergophobia, which is a fear of work? If so, be mindful of what you are working with. Another interesting phobia is nomophobia, the fear of being out of mobile contact. Many people appear to struggle with nomophobia.

Anxiety and fear are often used interchangeably, but they are not the same. One who is anxious is worried about something that could happen. One who is fearful might not necessarily be concerned about the future. Someone who is sitting at the desk about to take a certification exam may fear failing the exam but not be anxious about the future. Another person may fear the current exam and be anxious about the future if they fail.

Some people fear that they will be judged by other people. They do not take risks or think outside the box. A past client, Michael, was the oldest of four children, and he took on the role as the achiever among his siblings. During grade school and college, he always made good grades. He rarely caused his parents any problems. Michael became a board certified cardiologist. His career was all figured out, but his personal life was non-existent. He had a desire to go out and meet people but feared rejection. He feared that he would be seen as boring, so he didn't talk to people when he would go out. He didn't want to date online because he feared that no one would be interested in his profile. He was afraid that people would think that he was desperate for having to date online instead of meeting people through traditional means. Michael's fear prevented him from dating for years.

Mindful Acceptance helped Michael through this difficult time. Michael learned how to be mindful of his fearful thoughts that contributed to his isolating behaviors. He was creative and intentional about redirecting the energy from his fear of failure and rejection to engaging in more social settings.

Michael enjoyed specialty coffee. He began to frequent the same coffee shops to make small talk with people who shared his interests. He joined local meet-up groups based on activities that he enjoyed doing. Michael focused on his thoughts of hope and engaged in social situations that increased his self-confidence. Michael eventually met the love of his life and is now married with three children. He cultivated an active social life and felt more fulfilled.

Fear of abandonment

BAILEY WAS AN AVERAGE-LOOKING 25-year-old single woman with a slightly awkward body build. Her parents divorced when she was five years old, and she was raised by her mother. After the divorce, Bailey's father immediately started another family and did not maintain a relationship with Bailey.

Bailey came to visit me because of her romantic relationship. Her partner was ten years older and very demanding. Bailey acquiesced to most of her partner's wishes because she feared her partner leaving. When she did try to assert herself with her partner, he responded in a condescending and arrogant tone. Over time, Bailey began to feel undeserving of kindness, respect, and love. Bailey's fear of abandonment kept her in an unhealthy situation where her self-confidence and self-esteem were diminishing.

My work with Bailey focused on increasing awareness of her fear of abandonment. Her awareness of her abandonment issues allowed her to have compassion for her inner child that needed a little extra TLC. Bailey was intentional about either owning her decision to remain in her relationship or leaving. We identified fear-based thoughts and bodily sensations associated with it. Collaboratively, we determined what might work best for her, such as challenging and replacing the irrational thoughts or sitting with the thoughts, not agreeing with them, and moving forward with healthy self-affirming decisions. Working with Bailey reflects my emphasis on doing what works best for my clients. I do not use a cookie-cutter approach, assuming that any one method will work for everyone. I encourage my clients to do what works in their life, and flexibly choose how they want to move in this world.

Fear of being like your parent

MANY PARENTS DON'T REALIZE THAT they allow fear to dictate their behaviors with their own children. Many parents are so fearful that they will be like their own parents that they are being reactive instead of proactive with their children. Some adults are so unhappy with the way they were raised that they have vowed to parent their children differently.

I understand that many of us look over our childhoods and swear, 'I will never behave like him or her.' We can get so caught up in the vow that we overlook the bigger picture and the utility of our behaviors. Some parents are so fearful of behaving like their parents that they do the extreme opposite. Extreme is the operative word. Caution is encouraged whenever the pendulum swings from one opposite to the other. Here are some examples of extreme opposite behaviors:

- The child whose parent was overprotective and always treated like a baby is now a parent who is permissive and allows her child to do whatever he wants.
- A controlling and overbearing parent had parents who were hands-off.
- The parent who over-indulges her children with superficial things that had parents who were miserly.
- The child whose parent was unable to afford to put her in extracurricular activities is now a parent who has over-involved her children in too many activities.

VALERIE COMES FROM A PRIMARILY two-parent home where she did not have a healthy relationship with her mother who was physically absent for many years and overly religious, pretentious, and superficial. As a parent, Valerie is the exact opposite of her mother. She identifies as an atheist and doesn't have any interest in religious traditions, celebrations, or doctrines. Valerie is a helicopter mom. She follows her son wherever he goes. She does not attend family gatherings, and she doesn't put any effort into her appearance. She is the antithesis of her mother and doesn't even realize it.

Valerie is afraid that her son will grow up and not like her. She has inappropriately tried to be his best friend. Valerie needs to be mindful of her fears and issues with her own mother and begin to behave intentionally with her son—for her son's sake.

MY SUGGESTION TO ALL PARENTS is to be mindful and intentional in parenting. Time after time, I hear friends and acquaintances talking about giving their children what they did not have growing up. Often, people are referring to monetary and physical properties. I was recently talking to my partner about focusing on *what we did receive* in our childhood, not on *what we did not get* growing up. I did not grow up in a wealthy home. I did receive a lot of love and attention. I am very mindful that *things* do not build character, values, and morals. I am intentional about providing my children with character-building opportunities and positive experiences. I'm mindful and intentional about making sure that my children are given what worked for me, which was love, affection, and attention.

---

*Once we are aware of fear, we are able to make
a conscious and creative decision to use its energy
to motivate us to overcome whatever it is that we fear.*

IF YOU FEAR PUBLIC SPEAKING, use the nervous energy to motivate you to practice speaking in front of a mirror or join a Toastmasters group. If you fear looking for a job, use the nervous energy to practice mock interviews with a friend. If you fear taking tests, use the nervous energy to study for the exams. Don't allow the nervous energy to hinder you from making progress toward your goals. Fear is just misdirected energy, so let's redirect our energy and focus it where it can make a positive impact on our lives. When we transform a fear, we grow in emotional maturity and resiliency.

Best Self in Action: Irrational parenting fears

IT IS NORMAL FOR PARENTS to have irrational fears. We all do from time to time. We are better able to manage our irrational fears when we are aware of them. Awareness disengages automatic pilot and encourages intentional behavior. Use the questions below to gain insight into your internal world.

- Do you give your 2-year-old what he wants whenever he has a tantrum?
- Do you silence your child often?
- Do you have an issue with every person your son dates?
- Do you refuse to talk to your 12-year-old daughter about sex?

If you answered yes to any of the above questions, then you may want to be mindful of whether the situation is an irrational fear for you. Here is what the irrational fears look like, respectively:

- Your child will forever be angry with you, and you can't survive that thought.
- If you allow your child to voice controversial opinions, you will be encouraging her to be disrespectful to adults.
- You will be replaced by your son's partner, and your son will not love you anymore.
- Talking to your daughter about sex will 'cause' her to have sex and get pregnant.

PRACTICE BEING INTENTIONAL about noticing irrational thoughts and not taking them too seriously. If you find it difficult to not take the thought seriously, then be creative about trying other things, such as writing down the thought so you can see the irrationality on paper, recording yourself saying the thought, or imaging a friend saying the thought to you.

16

MINDFUL PARENTING

AWARENESS OF WHO YOU ARE AS A PERSON will help you understand who you are as a parent. Knowing who you are as a parent will influence your intentional parenting behaviors. If you are aware of your good, bad, and ugly, then you will engage in intentional parenting, which avoids passing down generational ways of doing things. For most of us, *when we know better, we do better.*

The three most researched parenting styles that have been postulated by Diana Baumrind are permissive, authoritarian, and authoritative. The permissive parenting style is relaxed and allows the child to do basically whatever she wants. This parenting style will easily give in to tantrums and demands from the child. The authoritarian parenting style is controlling and demanding. This parent would say to the child, 'Do as I say, not as I do.' This style sends the message that children *should* be seen and not heard. There would be zero tolerance for opinionated children. The last of Baumrind's parenting styles is the authoritative parenting style. This style combines warmth and care with a healthy balance between being permissive and authoritarian. This parenting style is intentional about meeting the child where he is developmentally.

Recently, another parenting style has gained some notoriety. A mother who uses an uninvolved or neglectful parenting style regularly tells her son to work out situations by himself without any parental involvement. Her son is strongly encouraged to be independent, not necessarily as an intentional act that best meets his needs, but as an automatic response that meets his mother's needs.

If your parenting style is working for you and your family, keep up the good work. If it is not working, identify your parenting style and its similarity to your upbringing. Increase awareness of your default parenting style, provide self-compassion to behaviors that have not worked, and be intentional and creative about engaging in thoughts and behaviors that are more constructive for you and your family.

Mindful and intentional parenting

THE CONCEPT OF MIRRORING was brought to my awareness after reading Shefali Tsabary's book, *The Conscious Parent*. I define the concept of mirroring as allowing your children and your relationship with your children to shine light on your unmet needs or mental knots and allowing this awareness to influence you to monitor and change your behaviors.

This mirroring concept was highlighted when a client, Riley, told me about a recent scenario. At the time, she had two daughters, ages four and two. One day, Riley's older daughter was disciplining her younger sister by aggressively yelling at her. Riley was very displeased with her older daughter's behavior. She was saddened with where she might have learned that behavior. *Could she have observed that behavior from me? No, that's just not possible. Something must be wrong with my 4-year-old. Her father must have allowed her to watch something too mature for her age on TV.*

Riley's defenses kicked in, and she wanted to blame someone or something for this behavior. She couldn't possibly look like that when she disciplined. After some soul searching, Riley realized that it was her behavior, and she needed to practice a fair amount of self-compassion because she was beginning to feel like a bad parent. Instead of taking her anger out on her older daughter for her blatant disrespect of her sister, Riley became intentional about modeling appropriate discipline and reprimanding behavior.

Mirroring slapped Riley in the face when her older daughter began to scold her father. Again, she was very displeased with her behavior because that was not an appropriate way to speak to her father. After stepping back and truly noticing the situation, Riley realized that she had to be intentional about changing her behavior towards her husband.

Encouraging children to do their Best

MY OLDER DAUGHTER TAUGHT ME the importance of allowing her to behave as her Best Self. Her personality is similar to her father's in many respects. They are both relatively reserved around people they do not know and reluctant to engage with people whom they don't know well. My mother tells me that my father and I have never met a stranger. I will talk to the person behind me in line at the store or next to me on the train. So, when my child appeared reluctant to open up to her peers and talk in new groups, I felt myself triggered and frustrated.

I thought that something might be wrong with my child. I had to realize that she had to come into her own at her own time. Over time, I've had to take a few steps back, take a few deep breaths, and realize that my child is not an extension of me. At a certain point, she began to describe herself as shy. I neither confirmed nor denied that label. I just explained what I observed, which was that she needed time to warm up to new people before she jumped right in. Interestingly, she has come out of her shell without any intimidation from me. Had

I pressured her to be a certain way, I might have increased her anxiety and created something in her that wasn't already there. I realized that when a parent demonstrates a lack of acceptance for a child's innate qualities, it is a violation of the child's ability to be her Best Self.

I HAD A PAST CLIENT, BERNARD, who refused to accept that his only son was not athletic. He forced his son to participate in sports that he did not enjoy. His son began to resent him, and their relationship became strained. Bernard once read his son's doodle paper, which was full of lightning bolts and zig-zag lines and screamed, 'I HATE my dad! He doesn't even see me.'

His son was creative and artsy; he thoroughly enjoyed art and drama classes. Bernard thought that creative endeavors were inappropriate uses of time. Initially, he thought that, like most parents, he was encouraging his son to use his time wisely. During Bernard's first few sessions with me, he explored his motivation to deny his son's natural strengths and attempt to force him to be someone he was not. Bernard increased his awareness of the importance of athleticism in his childhood. It was expected that all children in his household would be physically active, especially boys, because his father had been a professional basketball player and his mother was an amazing swimmer.

Bernard struggled with another reason why he was pressuring his son to be athletic. He secretly believed that to raise a heterosexual son, he must not expose him to art and 'girly' things. With much embarrassment, he said that he did not want to *make* his son gay. Bernard was provided a safe place to explore his beliefs. He struggled internally with the thought that if he did not push his son to be athletic, he was somehow grooming him to be feminine and to be attracted to boys. As irrational as this may seem, it was real for Bernard, and it was dictating how he behaved towards his son.

Bernard grew up in a religious environment where homosexuality was taught to be an abomination. Although Bernard didn't see himself as homophobic before having a son, he was now beginning to notice intolerant and oppressive thoughts that he appeared to harbor toward sexual orientation.

Bernard was beginning to hate himself for the pressure that he appeared to be putting on his son and the lack of connection between them. Bernard's mindfulness about his thoughts and behavior towards his son helped him to increase self-compassion. Bernard increased compassion for how difficult it must be for his son to receive messages that the way he was born wasn't good enough for his family.

Eventually, I was able to assist Bernard in deciding if his belief system was working for him and his son, not whether his beliefs were true or false. Bernard was assisted with identifying what he values most regarding a relationship with his son, and using this information to guide his interactions with him. Over time, Bernard and his son's relationship began to heal as Bernard increased his own awareness of his childhood messages and became intentional about respecting his son's individuality.

Our children are individuals who will have interests and desires that are separate from us. Raising children allows me to have a never-ending number of examples that illustrate that I am a work in progress, just like everyone else. Just in case my ego wants to make me think I am a better parent than most, something happens that brings me back to Earth, sometimes in the most embarrassing ways.

Modeling appropriate behavior as a parent

CHILDREN ARE TAUGHT BEST BY MODELING. Like many children, they were taught to 'do as I say not as I do.' This statement doesn't work. Most children do what their parents do.

One day, Beth and her son were on their way out of the house to soccer practice. He had asked her for $2.00 for the vending machine at soccer practice. Beth didn't have any cash at that moment, but she saw her husband's wallet and grabbed the money from there. Almost instantly, Beth realized that she was sending a message that it was ok to take without asking. She immediately suggested that they call upstairs and ask daddy if it was ok to borrow $2.00.

Beth was glad she caught that lapse in judgment, because later on if her son would take something that did not belong to him, he might say, 'Well, you take money out of dad's wallet.' Beth knew her response would be, 'But that's not the same.' It would have been unfair of her to be defensive. Instead, her son now has a good example to follow when he is in a similar situation in the future.

I TEND TO PICK FOOD OFF other family member's plate at dinnertime without asking, which is a habit of mine and one of my husband's pet peeves. Initially, I didn't think anything about it. Oddly, I thought it was a cute way of sharing. I guess, growing up in a household as the only child, I didn't learn that it was rude to pick food off other people's plates. Oh well, when you know better, you do better. After this issue had been brought to my attention by my husband who was raised with siblings and found it deeply disrespectful, I had to become intentional about the message that I was sending to my girls about boundaries and respecting other people's personal space. I had to change my behavior and realize that it was rude and inappropriate to take food or anything else from others without receiving permission.

For the most part, when people are young, they are unaware that they are learning certain behaviors. Many behaviors learned from parents are dormant and latent until people became a parent or engage in intimate relationships and instinctual parenting techniques appear to spontaneously occur. As a parent, I realized that my default and unconscious parenting skills were very similar to my immediate family's parenting style, which was to 'spare the rod and spoil the child.' Now, instead of 'spare the rod and spoil the child,' as my immediate go-to, I am very intentional in how I disciple and I primarily use very diverse corrective methods, such as removal of privileges, highlighting the positives, time-outs, and talks.

Highlighting the positives is a skill that I've found personal enjoyment with my children. At one point, especially when my girls were younger, they seemed to constantly engage in annoying and irritating behaviors, often related to antagonizing, comparing, or teasing each other. They just seemed combustible together. Given that I wasn't raised with other children in the house, I had a low tolerance for this type of conflict.

After I realized that it was normal for siblings to squabble, I became intentional about redirecting my attention from perceived negative behaviors. I adopted a mental star system, which was really more for me than for them. Whenever I would catch them engaging in appropriate and positive behavior, I would give them a verbal star and affirm that behavior. This star system allowed me to redirect my focus from the behaviors that annoyed me to behaviors that I had approved.

This star system wasn't fancy, but my girls really dug it. I explained to them that the reward system would begin anew every day, so the past would be in the past. If they earned three stars, then they would earn a mental eraser, which would allow them to erase a strike. So, strikes were given for inappropriate behaviors. Given that I really wanted my girls to win, I focused more on seeking appropriate behaviors and rewarding them. I didn't ignore inappropriate behaviors, but they were no longer my focus. My girls didn't get a treasure box at the end of the week. They did get a lot of words of affirmation, parental positivity, and fun times.

I'm not against parents boldly asserting themselves with their children. I encourage parents to be mindful and intentional about discipline. Be mindful of the type of discipline that you use when you are angry and when your emotional resources are low (when you are tired, hungry, stressed, or frustrated). During these most trying times, Mindful Acceptance is difficult to apply because most people do not have the energy or time to stop and think before they respond.

When people are exhausted, they just want to get things done, by any means necessary, including parenting and discipline. There is no judgment here. There is only compassion that I am sending your way. We have all been *there*, whatever *there* means for you. May your life be filled with opportunities to refuel and reenergize so that you can engage fully with yourself and others.

Setting realistic expectations

IT IS COMMON FOR PARENTS to experience over-attachments and unrealistic expectations for their children. Some children are forced to grow up too soon and take on inappropriate roles, being friends with their single parent, being 'the man of the house' at a young age, or acting as parents for their siblings.

Some single parents often think 'we all we got' when it comes to their children. I have a past client who had been a teenage mother. She became very good friends with her older daughter because her new baby had been her 'baby alive.' Their relationship became too enmeshed too soon. There was no room for the mother to discipline the daughter when the time came. There was not enough individuality between the two. Over time, the daughter grew to be very disrespectful towards the mother and the mother was at her wit's end, which is what brought her to see me. The mother was assisted with increasing her awareness of the nature of their relationship. She was assisted with exploring ways to fulfill her role as the mother and not the friend or sister.

HAVE YOU SEEN SITUATIONS where a single mother is raising a son and the son is expected to be 'the man of the house' at a young age? The son carries the burden of helping provide for his family rather than focusing on school and age appropriate play. Unfortunately, this young boy doesn't have the opportunity to experience his childhood because he becomes too focused on taking care of his family. This occurrence is rather common in low-income environments and the children turn to the streets and drugs for fast money.

Parents need to be mindful of placing unhealthy and unrealistic expectations on children and intentional about engaging in behaviors that respect the child's developmental age.

IN FAMILIES WITH MULTIPLE CHILDREN, the older children will often take on the role of caretaker for the younger children. The parent will inadvertently lean on the older children to be helpers. This is not necessarily a bad thing; it is just a thing to notice. Any behavior used in excess without attention to the situation could become problematic. In some cases, the flip side of the older child taking on extra responsibilities is that she typically blossoms into a mature adult. The darker, more extreme consequence could be the older child thinking that she is responsible for everyone around her. She could become an enabler and think it is her role to take care of everyone regardless to the situation. I am not implying right or wrong. I am just encouraging you to notice your behavior if you have multiple children and become intentional in engaging in value-consistent behaviors.

Best Self in Action: The mindful parent

DO YOU NOTICE YOUR OWN FEELINGS WHEN you are struggling with your child? If so, what have you noticed? Have you used what you have noticed to engage more mindfully and present-moment with your child? If not, the next time a conflict ensues between you and child, pause and notice what you are feeling and where in your body you are feeling this sensation.

Pausing and breathing before responding to your child can help during a difficult situation. This practice will help 'calm your nerves,' which means to relax your body, so that you can make emotional room to deal with what your child is saying and doing, without overreacting and behaving based off your overdriven emotions.

A mental body scan can be helpful, which is where you start with the top of your head and go down to your toes and notice whatever sensations are present. This body scan can help stabilize and ground your emotions so that you can see your situation clearly and make the best decision for you and your child in that moment of stress.

Do you notice what your mind is telling you during stressful interactions with your children? If so, do you always believe what it says? Remember that we have to hold lightly what our minds tell us. We have to notice our thoughts, and before behaving, ask ourselves, 'Is this behavior in the best interest of what I value and what I am trying to instill in my child?'

Conclusion: Your Best Self

THE FOUR DISCIPLINES OF MINDFUL ACCEPTANCE invite us to increase awareness of what is going on inside, outside, and around our bodies. This awareness pumps the brakes on the fast pace of life. *Mindfulness* of the present moment puts individuals in the position to take a sacred pause during everyday living. *Intentional actions* take life off autopilot. People can choose what is most important in life and commit to taking action, moving toward what they want their life to be about. *Self-compassion* is kind, gentle, soothing, and validating. Self-compassionate thoughts will decrease suffering and increase emotional stability, offering grace and forgiveness for past ineffective behaviors. *Creativity* opens up a world of possibilities. There are no limits to how high one can soar. Creativity allows individuals to transform the compost of life into beautiful flowers.

Mindful Acceptance may be challenging for some of us because practicing awareness might seem too painful. What do you do when reality seems overwhelming and unbearable? Most of us have a default response to ignore, distort, suppress, or repress pain. None of these solutions really work. These solutions are short-term remedies and Band-Aids on the real problem. The real problem is resisting what *is* and attempting to control automatic thoughts and emotions. As the saying goes, *the only way out is through*. Ignoring, distorting, suppressing, and repressing are all ways of trying to go under, around, and over the problem. There is no way around solving a problem without first bringing it into our awareness.

Many people think that they don't have time to engage in emotional self-care. Only when we engage in self-work, particularly emotional self-care, are we genuinely able to love and give to others unconditionally. Remember, we can't give what we don't have. Often, we give time to people and things that we value. We have to be mindful, intentional, self-compassionate, and creative about making time for ourselves in order to behave as our Best Self. Once we learn to take care of our basic emotional needs, we then will be able to give to others fully, willfully, and joyfully.

Some people refrain from emotional self-care because they think that it is selfish. Many of my clients have said, 'I feel so guilty doing nice things for myself and standing up for my needs.' I respond by asking, 'How do you feel when you do nice things for others?' The response is usually that they feel good. I then ask them to envision that their 'inner child' has needs, and doing nice things for themselves would be helping their inner child. Many clients are able to allow this concept to help them take better care of themselves without getting lost in their guilty thoughts.

Some people struggle with Mindful Acceptance and emotional self-care because of burnout. When we are burned out, we no longer have the emotional resources or emotional bandwidth to engage in intentional behaviors. The solution is to remember to practice Mindful Acceptance even if you don't feel like it; do it anyway in the service of doing what matters. Practicing Mindful Acceptance and doing what's important is *not* a matter of feeling or wanting. When we are burned out or overwhelmed, it is understandable that we are not going to want to do much of anything. When we do what is important to us, we often feel better and are glad that we engaged in the behavior although we did not initially feel like doing it. Motivation, energy, and pleasure will increase once we get started doing the things that are important to us.

Thoughts and emotions begin in our mind. As some *acceptance and commitment* therapists say, 'Our mind is not our enemy nor our friend.' Awareness of the way our minds have evolved to function is a key to happiness. Unwanted and intrusive thoughts will be broadcasted to us and uncomfortable emotions will occur. The secret is to notice without resistance these thoughts and emotions that are outside our control, with control being the opportune word. People want to get rid of internal private events by either moving away or towards certain behaviors.

I've heard people say, 'It's just easier to say yes and give in than to say no and deal with the uncomfortable emotions.' Try to remember that attempting to control the uncomfortable emotion by not asserting yourself and confronting the situation will only provide short-term relief. Long-term consequences in this situation often include resentment, pent up anger, and low self-esteem. An alternative to trying to avoid uncomfortable emotions is to notice the emotions, name what is being experienced, and then make emotional space for the energy so that it can come and go and rise and fall.

Try not to get caught up in judging, evaluating, and analyzing an emotion. Many people get tripped up when assigning meaning to an emotion. Just notice, name, and allow.

CONCLUSION

The intentional practice of Mindful Acceptance will help us be better partners in a wide variety of relationships. When you have taken care of your Self, you are able to assert yourself in the workplace by informing people of what you are willing and unwilling to do. You will be able to be present with your family and friends. If you are a parent, you will be able to give more of your Best Self to your children. Taking care of yourself will allow you to notice relationship patterns, persist with what works, and desist with what doesn't work.

By engaging in the four disciplines of Mindful Acceptance, people are better able to function with others with clear boundaries, authenticity, and genuineness. Adopting the skills of Mindful Acceptance will help people increase awareness of possible boundary violations, such as taking responsibility for other people's lives, become intentional about engaging in behaviors that are true to one's values, practice self-compassion, and increase creativity in problem solving.

Once we are able to mindfully accept who we are and where we are, we are positioning ourselves to go further. It is quite complicated, but that is how life works. Practice being mindful of accepting the *now*, whatever that may entail, and making the best of it. Interestingly, accepting the now opens the doors for new possibilities and opportunities for *later*. Once we are able to accept our present moments, it demonstrates to the God of our understanding that we are able to handle more, and more will come our way. More kindness, more patience, more love, more acceptance, more financial success, and healthier relationships is just a pebble in the jar of abundance that is awaiting us once we began to acknowledge and accept our realities.

What now?

NOW THAT YOU HAVE GONE ON THE JOURNEY of emotional self-care through practicing the four disciples of Mindful Acceptance, I would like to encourage you to take action based on what you value. Be aware that your values are what you choose, not what others think you should believe. In order to act in accordance with your values, you have to be aware of what you value.

The value of engaging in emotional self-care is often overlooked because physical self-care gets more attention. People can clearly see if you are not taking care of your outer shell. It is subtle as to whether a person is taking care of her inner landscape. If you think taking care of your mind, body, and soul is important, you might want to consider adding emotional self-care as a personal value. If you allow this value to guide your behaviors, you will be more likely to stand up for your beliefs, prevent being manipulated, assert boundaries, respect your time, space, and body, communicate effectively, enjoy life, accept your natural thoughts and emotions, and decrease the negative impact of intrusive thoughts and emotions. The practice of Mindful Acceptance will allow you to experience success in your internal and external worlds and live as your Best Self.

NOTES

Introduction

Aristotle. (2009). *The nicomachean ethics*. Translated by David Ross. Oxford World's Classics. Oxford: Oxford University Press.

Branch, Tara. (2003). Radical acceptance: Embracing your life with the heart of a Buddha. New York: Bantam Dell, 2003.

Gloster, A. T., Klotsche, J., Ciarrochi, J., Eifert, G., Sonntag, R., Wittchen, H., & Hoyer, J. (2017). Increasing valued behaviors precedes reduction in suffering: Findings from a randomized controlled trial using ACT. *Behavior Research and Therapy*, 91, 64-71.

Gloster, A.T., Meyer, A.H., Lieb, R. (2017). Psychological flexibility as a malleable public health target: Evidence from a representative sample. In press, corrected proof. *Journal of Contextual Behavioral Science*. Available online 20 February 2017.

Harris, R. (2008). The happiness trap: How to stop struggling and start living. Boston: Trumpeter.

Harris, R. (2009). Act made simple: An easy-to-read primer on acceptance and commitment therapy. Oakland: New Harbinger.

Hayes, S. C. (2004). Acceptance and commitment therapy, relational frame theory, and the third wave of behavioral and cognitive therapies. *Behavior Therapy*, 35, 638-665.

Hayes, S. C., Barnes-Holmes, D., & Roche, B. (Eds.). (2001). Relational frame theory: A Post-Skinnerian account of human language and cognition. New York: Plenum.

Hayes, S.C., Luoma, J., Bond, F., Masuda, A., & Lillis, J. (2006). Acceptance and commitment therapy: Model, processes, and outcomes. *Behaviour Research and Therapy*, 44, 1-25.

Lyubomirsky, S. (2007). The how of happiness: A new approach to getting the life you want. New York: Penguin.

Chapter Two

Hayes, S. C., Strosahl, K., & Wilson, K. G. (1999). *Acceptance and Commitment Therapy: An experiential approach to behavior change*. New York: Guilford Press.

Tolle, E. (2004). The power of now: A guide to spiritual enlightenment. Vancouver: Namaste.

Chapter Four

Altman, D. (2014). The mindfulness toolbox: 50 practical tips, tools, and handouts for anxiety, depression, stress and pain. Eau Claire, WA: PESI Publishing.

Hanh, T. (1991). Peace is every step: The path of mindfulness in everyday life. New York.

Kabat-Zinn, J. (2017). Defining mindfulness. Mindful: Taking time for what matters. Retrieved from http://www.mindful.org/jon-kabat-zinn-defining-mindfulness/.

Kabat-Zinn, J. (1994). *Wherever you go, there you are.* New York: Hyperion.

Neff, K. (2011). Self-Compassion: The proven power of being kind to yourself. New York: HarperCollins.

Chapter Five

Emmons, R. A. & McCullough, M. E. (2003). Counting blessings versus burdens: An experimental investigation of gratitude and subjective well-being in daily life. *Journal of Personality and Social Psychology*, 84, 377–389.

Harris, R. (2008). The happiness trap: How to stop struggling and start living. Boston: Trumpeter.

Helgeson, V. S., & Cohen, S. (1996). Social support and adjustment to cancer: reconciling descriptive, correlational, and intervention research. *Health Psychology*, 15 (2), 135-148.

The National Cancer Institute. (2014). Cancer support groups.

Rogers, C. (1961) On becoming a person: A therapist's view of psychotherapy. New York: Houghton Mifflin.

Chapter Six

Brown, B. (2010). The gifts of imperfection: Let go of who you think you're supposed to be and embrace who you are. Center City: Hazelden Publishing.

Grigoriadias, V. (2004, November 8). The Onlies: Only children are just like most New York kids— sophisticated, precocious, sometimes a little lonely—only more so. *New York Magazine.*

Sanders, A. R., Martin, E. R., Beecham, G. W., Guo, S., Dawood, K., Rieger, G., Badner, J. A., Gershon, E. S., Krishnappa, R. S., Kolundzija, A. B., Duan, J., Gejman, P. V., & J. M. Bailey (2015). Genome-wide scan demonstrates significant linkage for male sexual orientation. *Psychological Medicine*, 45, 1379-1388.

Chapter Seven

Luiz, D. M. (1997). The four agreements: A practical

guide to personal freedom. San Rafael: Amber-Allen.

Chapter Eight

Beattie, M. (1987). *Codependent no more: How to stop controlling others and start caring for yourself.* Center City: Hazelden.

Caprino, K. (2014, January 16). 7 Crippling parenting behaviors that keep children from growing into leaders. *Forbes.*

Chapter Ten

Allport, G. W. (1961). *Pattern and growth in personality.* New York: Holt, Rinehart, & Winston.

Chapman, G. (1992) The five love languages: The secret to love that lasts. Chicago: Northfield.

Dunn, E. W., Aknin, L. B., & Norton, M. I. (2008). Spending money on others promotes happiness. *Science* 21, 319 (5870), 1687-1688.

Hendrix, H. (2001). Getting the love you want: A guide for couples. New York: Henry Holt.

Kassin, S. (2003). *Psychology.* (4th edition) New York: Prentice-Hall.

Patrick, H. (2007) 'Do you want to do the dishes?' *Rochester Review* 69(5).

Chapter Fourteen

Baumrind, D. (1967). Child care practices anteceding

three patterns of preschool behavior. *Genetic Psychology Monographs,* 75(1), 43-88.

Tsabary, S. (2010). The conscious parent: Transforming ourselves, empowering our children. Vancouver, Namaste.

Appendix: About my Approach

My approach to Mindful Acceptance is a synthesis of the two scientific, evidence-based forms of psychotherapy: *cognitive-behavioral therapy* (CBT) and *acceptance and commitment therapy* (ACT). The four disciplines of Mindful Acceptance emphasize ACT perspectives, assumptions, and theories while flexibly using traditional CBT tools, such as increasing coping thoughts and positive affirmations.

Many approaches to living only focus on success in the external world such as in your career. My approach to living provides you with the skills and tools to experience success and happiness in your personal and career life. Mindful Acceptance extends from preparing to live a life of authenticity to living a life of purpose and meaning. Some people spend the majority of their life preparing and waiting on something to happen before living and loving life. I want to equip you with the tools to begin living, loving, and enjoying life right now. There is no time better than the Now.

Where Mindful Acceptance comes from

MINDFUL ACCEPTANCE IS A PSYCHOLOGICAL FORM of emotional self-care that allows every situation *to be what it is*, especially when we cannot change or control it. This approach is useful to us because we can't change or control most situations in life. We can increase our awareness of the nature of our thoughts and allow the private experience to take its natural course without any unnecessary struggle. Surrendering to the present moment allows us to clearly see the situation for what it is and choose the best possible response.

CBT emphasizes the importance of cognitions and utilizes behavior change interventions for the purpose of symptom reduction. This therapy proposes that dysfunctional thinking is the reason for psychological suffering. CBT strategies aim at behavior modification that directly attempts to change thoughts (Beck, 1995). Early in my profession, I had much success with using CBT as my primary form of therapy. The majority of my clients appeared to experience rather quick symptom reductions. I thought I had found a therapeutic elixir. Interestingly, a past client named Carrie who suffered from anxiety, was different. Like some of my other clients, she did respond quickly to the techniques of *cognitive-behavior therapy*. It appeared that over time, her symptoms would return and she would feel like a failure because she could not eliminate the unwanted thoughts and emotions. She had a difficult time understanding why she couldn't just get rid of her painful thoughts and emotions. Over time, she began to feel worse than she felt when she first began treatment. According to Carrie, time offered more proof that she was defective because she couldn't control her internal private experiences. Traditional CBT didn't work for everyone.

I continued to encounter clients like Carrie. Their resistance to a proven treatment puzzled me and my colleagues. I began exploring other therapy options to supplement *cognitive-behavior therapy*. Eventually, I found *acceptance and commitment therapy* (ACT), which had cognitive behavior roots and began introducing it to my clients. ACT is based on *relational frame theory*, which addresses human language and cognition. ACT is a revolutionary mindfulness-based approach to therapy that is being referred to as the 'third wave' in behavioral and cognitive therapy. Research suggests that many methods of CBT, such as comparing, analyzing, and evaluating that people use to solve internal problems can *cause* suffering. ACT teaches us to notice our thoughts, engage in mindfulness activities, and behave in ways that are consistent with our values.

ABOUT MY APPROACH

CBT and ACT have many similarities, such as noticing and naming thoughts. At the same time, there are significant differences. Unlike some branches of traditional CBT, which encourages us to identify, challenge, and replace our negative thoughts, ACT offers a different way of relating to uncomfortable thoughts. Instead of resisting and struggling with thoughts in an attempt to get rid of them, ACT encourages us to use mindfulness skills to learn to 'sit with' our thoughts and *act* in meaningful and effective ways.

ACT encourages us to learn to notice and observe intrusive or unwelcome thoughts without trying to make them go away. ACT discourages behaviors that attempt to remove or control uncomfortable thoughts and emotions because they cannot be permanently removed or controlled. According to the ACT model, suffering occurs when we resist what we cannot control, such as our unwanted thoughts and emotions. The alternative to resistance is allowing. The ACT technical term for this alternative to resistance is *acceptance*. Applying this understanding to my practice, I no longer talked about replacing automatic, irrational thoughts with rational thoughts. I began discussing different ways of relating to our thoughts and emotions. There was some confusion because many people wanted nothing more than to get rid of the intrusive thoughts and emotions that they had been working on dismantling.

The ACT model consists of six core therapeutic processes known to therapists as a hexaflex (from *hex* meaning *six*): defusion, acceptance, contact with the present moment, self as context, values, and committed action. These six interdependent processes work together to increase *psychological flexibility*, which according to Harris is the ability to 'be in the present moment with full awareness and openness to our experience, and to take action guided by our values.' Research has shown that psychological flexibility serves as a protective factor against daily stress and contributes to physical health, mental health, and well-being. Many of my clients were turned off and confused by any attempt to explain the ACT hexaflex didactically. I had to find a different way of exploring the six therapeutic processes without distracting folks with technical jargon.

Clients similar to Carrie began to benefit immensely once I was able to tweak the ACT hexaflex. I'm not the first person to tweak the hexaflex to make it workable for their clients. For instance, Kevin Polk and colleagues developed a tool called the ACT Matrix. Russ Harris developed the Choice Point that has the same goal of the ACT six psychological processes, which is to help clients increase psychological flexibility.

Upon analyzing feedback from my clients, I have found a way to integrate the ACT hexaflex into four disciplines that are easy for my clients to remember and apply to their lives.

The four disciplines of Mindful Acceptance are a condensed and palpable way of exploring ACT, which uses words that are familiar to most people: being mindful, intentional, self-compassionate, and creative. I have found that my clients can quickly learn these disciplines and effectively apply them every day of their lives, emotionally thriving in both mundane and challenging circumstances.

The four disciplines are firmly rooted in ACT. I've condensed four of the six ACT processes (defusion, acceptance, contact with the present moment, and self-as-context) into the disciplines of *mindfulness* and *self-compassion*. The other two ACT processes (values and committed action) are expressed in the disciplines of *intention* and *creativity*. Like the six ACT processes, the disciplines are interdependent, relying on each other in order to help people increase psychological flexibility and gracefully walk along their life journey.

ABOUT THE AUTHOR

DR. CHASITY K. ADAMS is a Licensed Psychologist, Health Service Provider, Life Coach, Speaker and Author in Charlotte, North Carolina. She is a member of the North Carolina Psychological Association, Mecklenburg Psychological Association, and Association for Contextual Behavior Science.

Dr. Adams received her doctorate in Clinical Psychology from Roosevelt University in Chicago, Illinois. During her graduate training, she focused on working with children, adolescents, and adults. She worked in diverse settings such as in a juvenile detention center, psychiatric unit of a hospital, community mental health center, and high school. She conducted an extensive amount of psychological and psychoeducational assessments during her training.

ABOUT THE AUTHOR

Dr. Adams completed her pre-doctoral internship at the University of North Carolina at Charlotte Counseling Center. Her post-doctoral training was completed at Dore Academy, a private school that specializes in working with children with learning and attention disabilities and the Charlotte Center for Balanced Living, which specializes in working with clients with disordered eating. Both of these experiences combined with her graduate training contributed to her wealth of knowledge in working with diverse clinical concerns and in diverse clinical settings.

Currently, Dr. Adams works in private practice as an independent practitioner. She specializes in helping people live as their Best Self by encouraging personal growth, habits of happiness, and emotional self-care.

If you would like to know more about Dr. Chasity K. Adams, please check out her website at www.drchasityadams.com and follow her on social media @drchasityadams on Facebook, Instagram, Twitter, and YouTube.

If you enjoyed this book, Dr. Adams would greatly appreciate an Amazon review.

Made in the USA
San Bernardino, CA
14 April 2019